W9-BWG-994

The Development of Hypothetico-Deductive Thinking in Children

A Cross-Cultural Study of the Validity of Piaget's Model of the Development of Logical Thinking

Kurt Bergling

University of Uppsala
and
Institute for the Study of International Problems in Education, University of Stockholm

Almqvist & Wiksell International
Stockholm

A Halsted Press Book
John Wiley & Sons
New York-London-Sydney-Toronto

Halsted Press ISBN 0 470-06972-2
Library of Congress Catalog Card Number 74-25170

Printed in Sweden by
TEXTGRUPPEN I UPPSALA AB, 1974

INTERNATIONAL ASSOCIATION FOR THE EVALUATION OF EDUCATIONAL ACHIEVEMENT (IEA)

IEA Monograph Studies No. 3

To Barbro

Contents

TABLES

Chapter 3

Chapter 4

FIGURES

Chapter 3

APPENDICES

Figures: Relative Frequencies and Trends of Ten Guttman Scales

Foreword

The data from the IEA Six Subject Survey were processed mainly at the IEA Data Processing Units at Columbia University, New York and at the University of Stockholm, respectively. The multivariate analyses for each of the six subject area reports were chiefly conducted at the Stockholm Data Processing Unit. With financial support from the Ford Foundation, it has been possible to build up a Data Bank in Stockholm which will be serviced by one statistician and one programmer; by the beginning of 1975 it will become available to *bona fide* researchers all over the world. Depositories of the bank will be placed at about half a dozen places outside Sweden.

The Spencer Foundation is financing a fellowship program, initiated in 1972 and continuing through the middle of 1977, which each year provides two post-doctoral and two pre-doctoral Fellows with the opportunity of conducting research at the Institute for the Study of International Problems in Education. Needless to say, the Fellows have welcomed the opportunity to have direct access to the IEA data. I should here like to mention particularly Dr. John Schwille who after his Spencer fellowship year stayed on with IEA as a research officer under the Ford Foundation Grant to supervise the preparation of the Data Bank and its accompanying codebooks.

The bank consists of master merged files for all the items and scores obtained in each subject area. Each student has been assigned the responses from his school in the school questionnaire which was completed by the principal and the mean responses made by the teachers to the teacher questionnaires from his school. Some quarter of a billion pieces of information have been entered onto 10 different types of merged files:

Science, Reading and Literature (Population I, 10-year-olds)
Science, Reading and Literature (Population II, 14-year-olds)
Science, Reading and Literature (Population IV, students in the pre-university grade)
English as a Foreign Language (Population II)
English as a Foreign Language (Population IV)
French as a Foreign Language (Population II)
French as a Foreign Language (Population IV)
Civic Education (Population I)
Civic Education (Population II)
Civic Education (Population IV)

The number of variables available in each subject area run close to a thousand in most files.

For each type of merged file a codebook has been prepared. It is, however, possible to tailor a codebook to match any subset of variables.

It has been considered important to present this condensed information about the Data Bank, because of the value for cross-national research that it represents. If one takes into account the time and other resources that have gone into the collection of this unique set of information on national systems of education, it is of utmost importance that they be made available to the international research community.

The investigation of the cross-national validity of the Piagetian model of the development of logical thinking conducted by Mr. Kurt Bergling is one illustration of the use that can be made of the Data Bank. In this case, item analysis information for two countries has been drawn upon, namely Sweden and India. As is pointed out by the investigator, the scope of the study could well be widened to encompass other subject areas and other nations with different socio-cultural structures. This would then also contribute to widening the perspective to other basic didactic problems, such as the cognitive prerequisites for the learning of various types of subject matter and how these "cognitive profiles" develop in different socio-cultural contexts. This should enable better teaching-learning strategies to be developed. By establishing valid measures of various aspects of logical thinking one could with better prospects of success begin to build models that would bring the field of didactics from the stage of an art to that of a science.

Stockholm, Institute for the Study
of International Problems in Education.

Torsten Husén
Chairman of IEA

Acknowledgements

For a number of years I have devoted myself to studies in concept learning, and I am now able to publish some results of my research in this field. Many people have helped me, in various ways, to carry out my investigations, and it is a real pleasure for me to thank all of them most heartily for their assistance.

In the first place, I wish to thank my teacher at the University of Uppsala, Professor Åke Andrén, who with his characteristic generosity has inspired and encouraged my research undertakings. In order to make possible inter disciplinary research related to theology and behavioral sciences he organized the joint efforts of the Theological Faculty of the University of Uppsala and the University of Stockholm's Department of Educational Research Stockholm School of Education, and Institute for the Study of International Problems in Education. The gratitude I feel for his help is due not only to his intellectual contribution but also to the friendship that has grown up during the past years.

At the Department of Educational Research, School of Education, fil.lic. Ingemar Fägerlind initiated the work and supported and encouraged me in my efforts. The problem faced in the present study has its roots in previous studies carried out within a research project (Project UMRe [Instructional Method–Religion]). Studies related to curriculum development in religion and to individualization of instruction in religion had been carried out within the theoretical framework of the Piagetian theory. Fägerlind, the leader of the project, inspired me to leave the field of applied research and focus on the corresponding problems of basic research, and he opened my eyes to the enormous possibilities of research based on the IEA Six Subject Data Bank.

I am also greatly indebted to Professor Torsten Husén, at the Institute for the Study of International Problems in Education, University of Stockholm. He generously invited me to carry on my studies within a research project of the International Association for the Evaluation of Educational Achievement (IEA), which meant that I had free access to the IEA Six Subject Data Bank as well as to stimulating and inspiring cooperation with research workers from Sweden at the Institute as well as from all over the world at the IEA International. As the leader of the IEA and my teacher during the past years, his role for my research work has been most important. His never-flagging interest, stimulating ideas and ability to solve problems have been an invaluable source of inspiration.

I am also deeply indebted to all my colleagues within the Institute and within the IEA- and UMRe-projects who have contributed at seminars and informal discussions. To all these project members I feel indebted for their cooperation and for the positive climate they created.

Fil. lic. Ingrid Mattsson and the data processing team have shown an untiring interest for my work and our cooperation has been stimulating. I will always be grateful for that.

With regard to the editorial work in connection with the dissertation, I have received great help from Mrs Clotye Larsson who has revised the English text, assisted in editing the volume and has also helped me in reading the proofs. I wish to thank her most heartily.

Finally, I wish to thank by beloved wife Barbro, who has helped and encouraged me and supported me in every possible way. To her the work is dedicated.

Stockholm, October 1974
Kurt Bergling

Abstract

An empirical study of both the construct and concurrent validity of the model of the development of hypothetico-deductive thinking proposed by Jean Piaget was conducted by applying this model to items from the IEA Six Subject Survey (Husén, *et al.*, 1973; Comber and Keeves, 1973).

The sample size was 918 Swedish boys, 880 Swedish girls and 1110 Hindi-speaking Indian boys. All the children were 120-131 months old.

The results confirm the basic proposition of the Piagetian theory—that is, that the development of thinking follows a predetermined fixed sequence of stages; and a cross-cultural comparison between Sweden and India confirms that the pattern is the same in both countries except for variation in rate.

It is demonstrated at the outset that item analysis data derived from multiple-choice items can be used in testing the validity of the Piagetian model of the development of thinking: that is, to predict answers in a meaningful way. Different methods of test construction based on the Piagetian theory were tried out. All scales and tests correlated higher with school achievement, as measured by the Science test (IEA/1A, 1B) than with two IEA verbal intelligence tests, the Word Knowledge test (IEA/2F) and the Reading Comprehension test (IEA/3C, 3D). This was interpreted as indicating that the Piagetian theory describes some type of "scientific" intelligence, rather than "verbal" intelligence, and that measures of this "scientific" intelligence are of importance to predict performance in school.

Descriptors:
Cognitive development, Concept formation, Intelligence measurement, International studies, Learning theory, Logical thinking, Piaget, Religious Education, Validity.

Chapter One

Introduction

A. BACKGROUND

The study of intellectual development according to Piaget's theory is being carried out all along the continuum from applied to basic research and with large differences in approach. Much applied research in education moves from the general to the specific, proceeding through such stages as (1) the study of intellectual development as a part of the analysis of student predispositions towards instruction; (2) the study of readiness for the specific subject matter field; (3) the development of teaching methods, and (4) evaluation. The reverse order is followed in basic research in education: one goes from the specific to the general in order to establish scientific principles or "laws" that might be of importance for instruction.

One example of a research project using both approaches for different studies was the one given the title UMRe, a Swedish abbreviation for Instructional Methods–Religion. The aim of the UMRe project was to investigate how the goals for instruction in religion could be implemented in a pedagogically suitable way. The project started in 1967 and was carried out at the Department of Educational and Psychological Research, School of Education, at the University of Stockholm, and financed by the National Board of Education. The project has dealt primarily with 10- to 12-year-olds. The chief goals of UMRe have been to investigate and analyze student predispositions towards instruction in religion, primarily studied within the theoretical framework of Piagetian theory, as well as to develop and test, in a limited way, units of instructional material.

The present author's area of concentration within the UMRe project involved research into readiness for instruction. In a study of concept formation (Bergling, 1971) about 100 experimental studies were reviewed. The logical analysis of stimuli and the sequence of stimulus presentation were of central importance in these experiments. Significant differences in difficulty in attainment of concepts representing ten conceptual rules of formal logic were found in a number of studies.

Previous studies of concept formation showed the importance of logic in concept formation and focused the author's attention on the problem of the development of logical thinking in the child. But before further work could be done, still another question had to be answered—where could suitable data for empirical study of this problem be found? The solution was provided by the International Association for the Evaluation of Educational Achievement (IEA), which generously offered me an opportunity to carry on my studies by using not only national Swedish data but also cross-cultural data from the Six Subject Survey. The data from this extensive survey in some 20 countries are now available in a Data Bank at the Institute for the Study of International Problems in Education, University of Stockholm.

The IEA, which was founded in 1967 as an autonomous, non-profit, non-governmental research organization, has conducted broad international surveys covering the main curricular areas of most national educational systems. Its aim has been to go beyond the purely descriptive into the formulation of internationally valid generalizations. Twenty-one countries have participated in the surveys, with between 8 and 19 countries taking part in each subject by testing at one or more of three age levels: 10-year-olds, 14-year-olds, and students in the last year of full-time secondary school. Since 1969 the IEA International staff, in charge of coordinating IEA-related research activities of the National Centers of the participating countries, are located at the University of Stockholm.

The Six Subject Survey was designed to make possible empirical testing of two types of specific hypotheses: first, hypotheses which are closely related to particular subject fields, and secondly, general hypotheses on the relationship between certain "input" factors and the outcome of the educational system. Uniquely, the survey made possible the testing of hypotheses not only across countries representing a wide variety of sociocultural patterns, but also across subject areas (Husén, 1974).

One of the fundamental psychological theories with far-reaching didactic implications that can be examined by means of IEA material is the theory of Jean Piaget. It describes the development of logical thinking[1] from childhood to adolescence in terms of a predetermined series of stages of thinking, making a sound distinction between the process of thinking and the objects of thinking; the *process of thinking* (the "general structures") according to Piaget always being the same regardless of varying *objects of thinking*, such as problems in different subject matter fields.

If this theory can be proved to be valid across social strata and cultures,

[1] The terminology of the present study will be as follows: *the development of logical thinking* refers to the maturational process described by Piaget in terms of his logical model; *stages of thinking* refer to the discrete stages in the model; *levels of thinking* will be used less precisely than stages of thinking, referring to measures of the development of logical thinking, not exactly referring to discrete stages, but to a continuum in the development. Scale types of the Guttman scales and test scores of the Thinking test and Reasoning Level test will be referred to as levels of thinking: *hypothetico-deductive thinking* and *propositional thinking* are synonums of *formal operational thinking*.

it can be expected to have an enormous impact on the didactics in all curricular areas, as it will be a further support for the individualization of instruction to fit the student's stage of thinking. The verbal interaction between student and student, as well as between student and teacher, will focus on helping pre-operational children (Stage 1) to develop into concrete operational thinking (Stage 2), as well as concrete operational children to develop into formal operational thinking (Stage 3), and formal operational children to become creative and inventive, going into unexplored areas of knowledge by means of their developing skill in hypothetico-deductive thinking. Finally, it will give a new dimension to school handicaps by making parents, teachers, and the students themselves aware that the maturational process goes on, enabling individuals to reach higher stages of thinking.

B. PURPOSES AND METHODOLOGICAL PROBLEMS IN THE STUDY OF VALIDITY

Jean Piaget's logical model of the development of hypothetico-deductive thinking, described extensively in his volumes on logical thinking (1949, 1950, 1956; Inhelder and Piaget, 1958, 1964) was an attempt at unifying the results of all his numerous experimental studies into a deductive theory. The ideal knowledge is seen as a deductive system in which all information is condensed into a few components, spelled out in a language as precise as that of logic.

In the context of such a theory the meaning of validity is that of verification. The study of validity focuses on the verification or falsification of predictions made on the basis of the theory.

Research based on such a theory is restricted to the limited number of steps which the maneuvering space of the theory allows. The logic and method underlying such research have been described by Brodbeck (1963). Some basic assumptions of the method may be noted here:

1. *Validity:* A concept is valid if it yields successful predictions. The measurement of validity is thus synonymous with accepting or rejecting specific hypotheses derived from the theory.
2. *Operational definitions:* There is a tautological character of definitions. An operational definition has the form of a conditional or an "if-then" sentence. If the number of conditions given in the definition of a construct is fulfilled, then the construct can be used instead of all the conditions.
3. *Model:* There is an assumption of a one-to-one relationship between the model and the area which it describes through a "translation" from a better-known area to a less-developed one.

C. STUDIES OF VALIDITY OF THE PIAGETIAN THEORY

No study *explicitly testing the validity of the logical model* of Jean Piaget has been found. This introduction shall therefore focus on some studies which do not set out to test the model directly but aim instead at validating some constructs used in the model.

Four groups of studies are of particular interest:

1. Studies of the validity of the hierarchical sequence of stages;
2. Studies of consistency in the child's behavior;
3. Studies of consistency between different parts of the Piagetian theory;
4. Studies of construct validity in tests using Piagetian tasks.

1. Validity of the Hierarchical Sequence of Stages

The hierarchical sequence of stages of thinking is at the core of the Piagetian theory. Most validation studies are concerned about accepting or rejecting this basic idea of the theory.

The methods used in a number of studies for testing the hypothesis of a unidimensional sequence of stages are based on the Guttman scale model (Guttman, 1944, 1950).

Schuessler and Strauss (1950) studied the development of the concept of "money" among 73 lower-class children and 68 middle-class children in Bloomington, Indiana, 4 to 13 years of age. They found that the items used formed a Guttman scale with a coefficient of reproducibility of 0.9. The development of the concept could be described by 11 scale types.

Strauss and Schuessler (1951) reexamined the 1950 study in terms of the logical operations of children at different ages. They found that the number of classes involved increases rather regularly as the items increase in difficulty; that the relationships between classes become correspondingly more numerous; that passing of more difficult items is, for the most part, based upon the simpler logical knowledge involved in passing simpler items; and that some of the youngest children cannot make propositions about a class, because the child has not yet learned the requisite logical operations which he needs to perform on the class and related classes.

In a more recent study in Geneva, Switzerland, of 35 boys and 37 girls equally divided among six age levels by half-year intervals from ages 4:0 to 7:0, Wohlwill (1960) found support for Piaget's theoretical views of a relatively uniform developmental sequence in the area of number concept. He saw evidence for the existence of three fairly sharply-differentiated stages in the development of the number concept: an initial, preconceptual stage, in which number is responded to purely in perceptual terms, without any symbolic mediation; an intermediate stage, in which the mediating structures representing individual stimuli on this dimension are developed so that the perceptual support necessary for generalization between two equivalent stimuli on this dimension is steadily reduced; and a final stage, in which superordinate structures, representing the number concept in the abstract and relating the individual numbers to each other, are elaborated, thereby leading to an understanding of such fundamental principles as the conservation of number and the coordination between ordinal and cardinal number.

Mannix (1960) made a replication of eight of the tests described by Piaget (1952) in *The Child's Conception of Number*. The aim of the Mannix research was to discover whether E.S.N. children behaved similarly to or different from the normal children tested by Piaget in the construction of certain concepts of number and quantity. Forty-eight E.S.N. children, representing a range of mental ages from 5 to 9 years, were tested. Mannix found evidence for a "preconceptual" stage (Stage 1) and an "operational" stage (Stage 3) with children's responses very similar to those quoted by Piaget. But the evidence for an intermediate stage ("period of intuitive thought") was less convincing. Scalogram analysis based on only the two categories, "Operational" responses and "Pre-Operational" responses gave a coefficient of reproducibility of 0.94, leading Mannix to the conclusion that the behavior of E.S.N. children in the construction of certain number concepts is, on the whole, similar to that of the normal children tested by Piaget; and that the period of development from the first to the third stage corresponds to a span of mental age of 5 to 8 years. The absence of evidence of an intermediate stage was interpreted to mean either that such a stage does not exist or was due to a lack of discrimination of the test.

Using Piaget's semi-clinical method in a study of 250 children, from 5:1 to 10:1 years of age, Dodwell (1960, 1961) set out to assess the generality of the types of behavior that Piaget calls the stage of global comparison, the intuitive stage, and the concrete operational stage. Scalogram analysis with Goodenough's modification of the Cornell technique was used, and a coefficient of reproducibility of only 0.690 was obtained, showing at best a "quasi-scale."

The following year (1962) Dodwell studied 60 children, between the ages of 5:2 and 8:8 years, in order to examine the relationship between two types of problems which according to Piaget develop together and form a single system: the construction of number and the development of simple class logic. The "logic" questions and the "number concept" questions were found to form a single Guttman scale, but the coefficient of reproducibility obtained was as low as 0.6 and thus formed, at best, a "quasi-scale." The pattern of development was neither as regular, nor as simple, as Piaget has suggested.

Zern (1969) found in his reexamination of Smedslund's (1963) data on the development of concrete reasoning in 160 children, ranging in age from 4 to 11 years, that the data form a Guttman scale with a coefficient of reproducibility of 0.923.

Schwartz and Scholnick (1970) tested out on 32 girls and eight boys, between the ages of 53 months and 76 months, the hypothesis that conservation requires a series of judgments: (1) direct comparison, (2) identity judgment, and (3) equivalence judgment. The ability to make these three judgements may develop sequentially, with the simplest comparative judgment being a prerequisite for dealing with the effects of a transferral, and with the acceptance of invariance in the identity of the transferred object being a prerequisite for equivalence judgments. Schwartz and Scholnick found that the seven items with nonverbal tasks formed a Guttman scale. Age, stimulus variables, and the medium of response (verbal versus nonverbal) affected the relative difficulty of the conservation tasks.

2. Consistency in the Child's Behavior

A special type of validity studies focuses on the degree of convergence of indicators. Individuals who score high on tests using interval data ought to score high on other indicators of the same construct. Studies of Piagetian tasks, which classify individuals on discrete levels of thinking, would expect consistency between various tasks in the child's behavior. None of the indicators is thereby taken as a criterion or standard. Low intercorrelation casts doubt on all the measures.

In a study of convergence comprising 250 children ranging in age from 5:1 to 10:1 years, Dodwell (1960) examined the consistency of behavior on five types of tasks (relation of perceived size to number; provoked correspondence; unprovoked correspondence; seriation; cardination and ordination). He classified the children on three stages: the stage of "global comparison"; the intuitive stage; and the stage of conrete operations. He found that a child may be in Stage 1 for one type of material and situation, and in Stage 2, or even 3, for another; hence it is impossible to state a "typical" age for the attainment of concrete operational activity. Although a child can be assigned with a fair degree of assurance to one of the three categories for each test subgroup, there is no consistency of stages within individuals, nor are the age trends similar for the different subgroups.

Dodwell (1962) reports similar results in his comparison between number concept questions and the development of simple class logic, which is discussed in the section below.

3. Consistency between Different Parts of the Theory

Convergence studies may also be applied to a theory. If the theory postulates that two different types of problems develop together and form a single system, then the convergence of indicators will not only measure the relationship between these two problems but make possible a test of the theory itself.

In the investigation mentioned above, involving 60 children between the ages of 5:2 and 8:8 years, Dodwell (1962) studied the relationship between two types of problems which according to Piaget develop together and form a single system: the construction of number and the development of simple class logic. The construction of number was measured by the Number Concept Test. The construction of simple class logic was studied by using different sorts of objects: dolls, toy gardening tools, toy cars.

The actual relationship investigated by Piaget (1952) and by Dodwell (1962) was the child's understanding of the fact that two groups of "things," such as a group of boys and a group of girls, together constitute a single, larger, group of children, and that the total group of children is the "additive composition" of the smaller groups. In the normal set notation: $B \cap G = C$. The actual relation investigated by Piaget was this: given these two relations does the child understand that $B < C$, or $B = C - G$? Result: Just as he did in his Number Concept Test (1960), Dodwell found that the answers to the logic problems could be divided into three groups, classified as "global comparison" (scored 1), "intuitive judgment" (scored 2) and "operational judgment" (scored 3).

Dodwell's convergence study seems to indicate that understanding of the nature of hierarchical classification develops to a large extent independently of understanding of the concept of cardinal number. The correlations between answers about composition of classes and about number concepts were low; most of them were, in fact, insignificant.

The "logic" questions and the "number concept" questions form a single Guttman scale, but the coefficient of reproducibility was as low as 0.6 and thus formed at best a "quasi-scale." The pattern of development was neither as regular, nor as simple, as Piaget has suggested.

4. Construct Validity in Tests using Piaget's Tasks

Test validation, as described by Cureton (1951), Cronbach and Meehl (1955) and Cronbach (1971) is the process of examining the accuracy of a specific prediction or inference made from a test score. One important type of test validation, which is closely related to validation of a scientific theory, is construct validation.

An example of construct validation is to be seen in the work of Raven (1973) who wished to ascertain whether the items on his Ravens' Test of Logical Operations (RTLO), actually measured the logical operations for which they were designed. He used five judges, each of whom was professionally involved with Piaget's work and each of whom had completed an empirical study of logical thinking for his doctoral degree. He reports a 100 % agreement among the judges.

Factor analysis is frequently used in construct validation. Tests that by hypothesis are indicators of a certain construct are expected to show substantial loadings on the same factor. With loadings on a second factor the indicator is shown to be impure. A similar anomaly occurs if a test that is not supposed to represent the construct loads on the factor linking its indicators.

Factor analysis was employed by Goldschmid and Bentler (1968) in a study of the dimensions of conservation. Their findings, that conservation of length is completely uncorrelated with conservation of distance, led them to the conclusion that Piaget's theory is in need of revision.

Raven (1973) used factor analysis to study the factor pattern for seven major groups of logical operations (classification, seriation, logical multiplication, compensation, probability, correlation, and proportional thinking). The pattern showed that all, except seriation, are discrete factors. The second factor is loaded in the following four subtests: seriation, logical multiplication, compensation, and proportional thinking. Raven explains the second factor by the logical relationship between the four subtests. Seriation is closely related to logical multiplication because the ability to construct co-univocal logical operations depends upon the ability to coordinate two serially changing variables. Compensatory and proportionality operations require the reciprocal ordering or seriation of variables.

Raven makes no attempt at relating performance on his test, RTLO, to the discrete stages of thinking in Piaget's logical model, but Raven's second factor could perhaps be interpreted as favoring Piaget's claim that logic can be used as a model of thinking.

Chapter Two

Problem

A. THE THEORY

Jean Piaget regards his logical model as a deductive theory based on findings in experimental psychology. He describes the objectives of formulating his model as being "to construct by means of the algebra of logic a deductive theory to explain some of the experimental findings of psychology" (Piaget, 1956, p. 26). A concise summary of the logical model has been given by Piaget (*ibid.*, pp. 26–37).

1. Definitions

Pre-operational thinking is negatively defined as thinking without reversibility. Reversibility is defined as the permanent ability of returning to the starting point of the operation in question.

Concrete operational thinking is defined as the thinking that is capable of two-way classification. Four groupments of classes and four groupments of relations express the totality of operations at the psychological level of concrete operations. The table of four concrete operations is isomorphic with a truth-value table with 2 x 2 cells, with groupments made two at a time.

Formal operational thinking is defined as propositional thinking, capable of n-way classification. Sixteen propositional operations, in the case of binary operations, and 256 ternary operations express the totality of operations at the psychological level of formal operations. The table of 16 propositional operations is isomorphic with a truth-value table for two propositions, in which all the possible products are listed.

2. Postulates

Postulate 1: The development of thinking follows a predetermined fixed sequence of stages: pre-operational thinking, concrete operational thinking, formal operational thinking.

Postulate 2: The rate at which the child progresses through the developmental succession may vary, especially from one culture to another.

B. THE PROBLEM

The specific objectives of the present study were to investigate the construct and the concurrent validity of the logical model of the development of logical thinking proposed by Piaget, by applying this model to a selection of IEA items.

Problem 1: To test whether the development of thinking indeed follows a predetermined fixed sequence of stages: pre-operational thinking, concrete operational thinking, and formal operational thinking.

Problem 2: To test whether the development of thinking follows the same pattern except for variation in rate in two very different cultures, by means of a cross-cultural comparison between Sweden and India.

Problem 3: To try out different ways of test construction based on the Piagetian theory: one indirect approach by means of a series of Guttman scales, and one direct approach based on individual items.

Problem 4: To study whether and to what extent the level of development of logical thinking is positively correlated with school achievement.

Problem 5: To study whether and to what extent the different levels or stages of thinking discriminate between different levels of performance.

Problem 6: To find out whether Piaget has described a type of "verbal intelligence" or a type of "scientific intelligence," which he himself refers to as "operational intelligence."

C. HYPOTHESES

Hypothesis 1: The predetermined fixed sequence of stages in the development of logical thinking (pre-operational thinking, concrete operational thinking, formal operational thinking) will allow scalogram analysis.

Hypothesis 2: The cross-culturally uniform developmental sequence of stages in the development of logical thinking will fit the same Guttman scales in both Sweden and India.

Hypothesis 3: Different methods of test construction based on the Piagetian theory (an indirect approach through a series of Guttman scales, and a direct approach based on individual items) will be highly correlated with each other if the theory-oriented item analysis is valid.

Hypothesis 4: The Guttman scales as well as the two tests mentioned above (3) will be positively correlated with tests of school achievement.

Hypothesis 5: One-way analysis of variance and test of linearity of the Guttman scales, with the IEA tests (Word Knowledge, Reading Comprehension, Science) as dependent variables, will show significant differences between the scale types (i.e., different levels of the development of logical thinking) as well as linear trends.

Hypothesis 6a: If the Guttman scales and tests do measure some type of "verbal intelligence" they will show higher correlations with the verbal intelligence tests (Word Knowledge, Reading Comprehension) than with the Science test.

Hypothesis 6b, alternative hypothesis: If the scales and tests measure some other type of intelligence of particular importance for "scientific thinking" they will show higher correlations with the Science test than with the two verbal intelligence tests.

Chapter Three

Method

A. SYNOPSIS OF THE STUDY

The present study was conducted in three major series of analyses: (I) Analyses of importance for decisions about adequacy of the data set used; (II) Analyses of importance for the method used; and (III) Analyses using the methods developed for testing the six hypotheses advanced about the validity of Piaget's Logical Model, reported in Chapter Four, "Results." Analyses I and II are reported in Chapter Three, "Method."

I. At the beginning of the study a decision had to be made about which subjects to study. Two problems had to be considered, the possible existence of illiteracy and of groups of "different thinking" students in the samples. Finally, the effects of changing the data set had to be investigated, especially the effects on the estimates of the reliabilities of the IEA tests.

II. A series of analyses of single items had to be carried out before analyses of more than one item at a time for scale- and test-construction could be done.

A. Analyses of single items were used in order to get answers to three problems:

(a) first, the basic question had to be answered: Can multiple-choice items be used in studies of Piagetian problems?, as the whole study was planned to be based on such items;

(b) secondly: How good are the items for the purpose of the study? Three types of item analyses were carried through in order to answer question (b): first, the conventional inspection of item difficulty and discriminating power; secondly, a new method of criterion-related item analysis, and thirdly, a new method of theory-oriented item analysis.

(c) Finally, a separate study had to be conducted, focusing on the reliability of the classifications of distractors on stages of thinking.

B. The analyses of single items were followed by analyses using more than one item at a time for scale- and test-construction: (a) the construction of ten Guttman scales; (b) the construction of a Thinking test; (c) the construction of a Reasoning Level test.

III. The methods, developed through the procedure described in Chapter Three, "Method," were then used for solving the main problem of the study: testing six hypotheses on the validity of Piaget's Logical Model.

A synopsis of the entire study will thus be as follows:

I. Analyses of importance for decisions about the data set used
   A. General considerations
   B. Some problems of the IEA data set
      1. illiteracy
      2. "different thinking"
   C. Effects on estimates of reliabilities of IEA tests when using a restricted sample, eliminating certain groups from the IEA sample

II. Analyses of importance for the method used
   A. Analyses of single items
      1. The basic question: can multiple-choice items be used in studies of Piagetian problems?
      2. Three types of item analysis
         a. difficulty and discriminating power
         b. criterion-related item analyses
         c. theory-oriented item analysis
      3. Study of reliability of classifications of distractors on stages of thinking

   B. Analyses of more than one item at a time for scale- and test-construction
      1. Construction of ten Guttman scales
         a. scale construction
         b. studies of reliability of the scales
      2. Construction of the Thinking test
      3. Construction of the Reasoning Level test

III. Analyses using the methods developed for testing the six hypotheses of the study

B. THE DATA SET USED

1. General Considerations about the Study and the Data Set

When the present study was designed nobody knew if the validity of the Piagetian theory would have any chance of being tested by means of IEA items, because these items had been primarily constructed for the purpose of an international evaluation of educational achievements (Bloom, 1969, p. 1). For three reasons it appeared that the 40 items in the Science test at the 10-year-old level (IEA/1A, 1B) probably would have to be reduced considerably. First of all, since an investigation of the Piagetian theory had not been an objective in IEA's test construction, it was uncertain whether there would be any "Piagetian" tasks in the test. Secondly, some items would have to be eliminated in the process of changing multiple-choice items with one right and four wrong alternatives into a scale, ignoring the right-wrong dichotomy in favor of a classification of the distractors into three hypothetical stages of thinking. Not all items could be classified in this way. Thirdly, the few items left must be of sufficiently high quality on all distractors in order to discriminate between the hypothesized stages of thinking.

One basic idea of how to prove or disprove the Piagetian theory was, at this early stage of the study, the assumption that the type of intelligence studied by Piaget would be positively correlated with other intelligence tests. Two verbal intelligence tests were available within the IEA data set, the Word Knowledge test (IEA/2F) and the Reading Comprehension test (IEA/3C, 3D). This second measure would also be necessary for control of the possible existence of illiteracy in the sample (Thorndike, 1973, p. 55).

Thus, it was decided that the Word Knowledge test (IEA/2F) and the Reading Comprehension test (IEA/3C, 3D) should be used to enable the author to examine the relationships between the Piagetian stages of thinking and verbal intelligence. It was further decided that the Reading Comprehension test should be used to control all testees for illiteracy.

For a cross-cultural validation of the Piagetian theory, the optimum condition would be to examine samples from countries maximally different in language and culture. For this pilot study Sweden was chosen to represent the "developed" highly industrialized West European culture. The best sample from the developing nations available within the Six Subject Data Bank was that composed of Hindi-speaking Indian boys.

In the present study, the minimum requirements for inclusion of an individual in the data set were these:

1. Answering at least four out of the seven "Piagetian" problems in the Science test (IEA/1A, 1B) which had been found in a preliminary analysis of this test;
2. Participation in the Word Knowledge test (IEA/2F);

3. Participation in the Reading Comprehension test (IEA/3C, 3D).

Nine hundred eighteen Swedish boys, 880 Swedish girls and 1110 Hindi-speaking Indian boys, aged 10:0—10:11 years at the time of testing, were found to fill these three minimum requirements.

A comprehensive technical report on the sampling procedures and methods used in the IEA Six Subject Survey is given in *An Empirical Study of Education in Twenty-One Countries: A Technical Report* (Peaker, forthcoming). The sampling procedures used are also described in Comber and Keeves (1973, pp. 43—50), Husén, *et al.* (1973, pp. 36—44).

Two more problems had to be considered before decisions actually could be made about which students to study:

1. The definition of illiterates, to be used for elimination of illiterates from the sample, had to be refined. This does not mean that the IEA definition of the population was changed, for both illiterates and literates had the same chance of being sampled. But it will result in the formulation of the definition of the restricted sample used in the present study, setting necessary restrictions on the inferences that can be made from the sample used in this pilot study.

2. How to handle the "none-of-these" option in item IEA/1A:16 had to be decided.

2. Definitions of Illiterates

Correction for guessing was carried through on all tests using the conventional formula:

$$R - \frac{W}{k-1} \qquad (1)$$

where: R = number of correct answers
W = number of wrong answers
k = number of alternatives in multiple-choice items

This formula allows for a score of 0.0 by random guessing. In a first attempt to arrive at an operational definition of illiteracy, illiterates were defined as those who in the Reading Comprehension test (IEA/3C, 3D) did not achieve a total corrected score higher than 0.0.

Tables 3.1 and 3.2 show the data set used in this study grouped by literacy, sex (in Sweden), and grade.

Table 3.1. *The Sample of the Present Study, Sweden, Grouped by Literacy, Sex and Grade. (Percentage in brackets)*

Category of Students Literacy	Grade	Number of Individuals Boys	Girls
Literates RCC >0.0	3	422 (94.8)	408 (98.6)
	4	467 (98.7)	462 (99.1)
	Total	889 (96.8)	870 (98.9)
Illiterates RCC ⩽0.0	3	23 (5.2)	6 (1.4)
	4	6 (1.3)	4 (0.9)
	Total	29 (3.2)	10 (1.1)

Table 3.2. *The Sample of the Present Study, India, Grouped by Literacy and Grade (Percentage in brackets)*

Category of Students Literacy	Grade	Number of Individuals Boys
Literates RCC >0.0	3	174 (76.3)
	4	301 (80.9)
	5	326 (87.2)
	6	98 (72.1)
	Total	899 (81.0)
Illiterates RCC⩽0.0	3	54 (23.7)
	4	71 (19.1)
	5	48 (12.8)
	6	38 (27.9)
	Total	211 (19.0)

Table 3.3. *Comparison between Coefficients for Scales using Two Different Criteria for Exclusion of Illiterates, India*

Scale	Criterion	Coefficients 1	2	3	4
GUTSC1A	RCC> 0.0	.810	.641	.130	.406
	RCC>10.0	.812	.681	.131	.411
GUTSC1B	RCC> 0.0	.823	.646	.178	.501
	RCC>10.0	.825	.646	.179	.505

Coefficients:
1 = coefficient of reproducibility
2 = minimum marginal reproducibility
3 = percent improvement
4 = coefficient of scalability

A score just above 0.0 might be regarded as a very liberal criterion of literacy, and in order to control the effects on the Guttman scaling, it was decided to rescale the two scales, GUTSCIA and GUTSCIB, using a higher score on the criterion than 10.0. Table 3.3 shows the very small differences in the coefficients which resulted from the change to a higher score on the criterion. In the light of these results, it seemed wise to use the lower score on the criterion which enabled us to study as large a sample as possible.

3. Missing or "Different Thinking"

Item IEA/1A:16 has a "none-of-these"-option as distractor E. This item was regarded as the most important in this study. It was the item by means of which the theory-oriented item analysis was developed and its usefulness tested. This item was included in all Guttman scales. The treatment of a "none-of-these"-option in this item therefore deserves particular attention.

A "none-of-these"-option appears twice in the Science test (IEA/1A, 1B). The first such option is in exercise item 1 that preceeded the actual test. The second use is made in IEA/1A:16. Because of the use of this type of option in the first exercise item, testees probably regarded this as a real option having the same chance of being the right answer as any other.

The instruction used in introducing the test (IEA/1A, 1B) reads as follows:

> "Each of the questions or unfinished statements in this test is followed by five suggested answers, lettered A, B, C, D or E. You have to decide which *one* answer you think best and then on your answer card make a solid pencil mark in the oval containing the correct answer letter."
>
> (Manual for Test Administrators, IEA/M3)

Ebel (1951, p. 237) and Wesman (1971, p. 117) regard this type of option as useful when testing in fields where conventions of correctness can be applied rigorously, such as in items in arithmetic. But they regard it as inappropriate in best-answer items. According to the instruction, the items in the Science test are "best-answer items."

Wesman and Bennet (1946) investigated the use of "none-of-these" as an option in a vocabulary and in an arithmetic test. They found no difference, on the average, in difficulty or in correlation with an external criterion, when "none-of-these" was substituted for the answer or for one of the other options in tests given in two forms to matched groups.

The choice of item type is closely related to the objectives of the testing.

The "none-of-these"-option might well have worked properly in the Science test, which has one right answer to this question. But for the purpose of the present study it was impossible to analyze this option in terms of hypothesized stages of thinking.

An open question for future research will be to see whether the group of students who chose this "none-of-these"-distractor are representatives of some type of "different thinking" not described by the Piagetian theory, or might as well be regarded as "missing" on this item. Until the hypothesis of "different thinking" can be rejected, this group of students will be eliminated from the analyses as "different thinking."

Table 3.4 shows the number of "different thinking" students, illiterates excluded.

Table 3.4. *"Different Thinking" Students (RCC > 0.0) Grouped According to Nationality, Grade and Sex (Percentage in brackets)*

Category of Students Nationality	Grade	Number of Individuals Boys	Girls
Sweden	3	35 (7.9)	65 (15.7)
	4	28 (5.9)	47 (10.1)
	Total	63 (6.9)	112 (12.7)
India	3	25 (11.0)	
	4	43 (11.6)	
	5	34 (9.1)	
	6	9 (6.6)	
	Total	111 (10.0)	

4. The Sample

When the illiterates were removed from the sample–illiterates being defined as individuals with a total corrected score of $\leqslant 0.0$ in the Reading Comprehension test (IEA/3C,3D)–the final group actually used in all scaling and test construction was comprised of 889 Swedish boys, 870 Swedish girls and 899 Indian boys.

C. TEST INSTRUMENTS I: SOME IEA TESTS

Three IEA tests were chosen for the present study:
1. Science I–Section A and Section B (IEA/1A, 1B)
2. Word Knowledge Test–Section F (IEA/2F)
3. Reading Comprehension–Section C and Section D (IEA/3C, 3D)

The corresponding data bank numbers for the tests are:
1. IEA/1A = ElSA and IEA/1B = ElSB
2. IEA/2F = El5W
3. IEA/3C = ElRC and IEA/3D = ElRD

The possibilities of constructing internationally applicable cognitive instruments to evaluate the outcomes of learning, which would be the basis for further work on international evaluation of educational achievement, were examined in a pilot study in 13 countries (Foshay, 1962). These findings were the starting point for development of test instruments for the Mathematics Study (Husén, 1967) and the Six Subject Survey. The test construction for the Six Subject Survey was a separate research project, going on from 1966–69, during which international committees in cooperation with the National Centers constructed and pretested the instruments (Bloom, 1969; Husén, 1974).

The procedure to be followed at the testing was set out in detail in the test manual. The three tests were given at three different sessions, the sequence of which was regarded as important. Science I (30 + 30 minutes) was given at the beginning of Session 1 (85 minutes). The Word Knowledge Test (10 minutes) was given at the beginning of Session 2 (35 minutes). The Reading Comprehension Test (25 + 25 minutes) was given at the beginning of Session 3 (60 minutes). None of these tests was regarded as a speeded test. The time limits were purely administrative.

Four measures from these tests are used in the present study: total corrected scores of the three tests, and total corrected score of a Minimized Science test (Science I with the seven items of this study eliminated). No attention is paid to the different subtests of Science I and Reading Comprehension.

Reliability coefficients, in this case Kuder-Richardson 20, for these tests are reported in the Six Subject Survey. But, as it might be expected that the differences between the samples used in that study and in the present one would also affect the reliability coefficients, a new set of coefficients was computed. It was expected that the direction of changes would be slightly lower in the present study, because the variance of the tests would be minimized by excluding those low-achieving students classified as illiterates. A comparison between the two sets of coefficients is given in Table 3.5.

Table 3.5. *Comparison between Reliability Coefficients Computed on the Six Subject Survey (including Illiterates and Partial Missing) and the Sample of the Present Study (excluding these)*

Test	Study	Reliabilities (KR–20)	
		Sweden	India
Science I (IEA/1A, 1B)	Six Subject Survey	.79	.84
	The present study	.78	.83
Reading Comprehension (IEA/3C, 3D)	Six Subject Survey	.88	.84
	The present study	.88	.76

D. THE BASIC QUESTION: CAN MULTIPLE-CHOICE ITEMS BE USED IN STUDIES OF PIAGETIAN PROBLEMS?

1. Introduction

The predominant method of testing Piagetian problems has been the "semi-clinical" or interview method introduced by Jean Piaget. An area of investigation still by and large unexplored is the construction of questionnaires for group testing of development of thinking in terms of the theory of Piaget.

One of the pioneer efforts in using the questionnaire approach was that of Tisher (1971), who succeeded in constructing a paper-and-pencil test for group testing, instead of the ususal interview method. He compared classifications based on the questionnaire with those based on the interview method and found a 77 % agreement.

Assessment of the correlation between performance in a Piagetian "standard" experiment and performance on a corresponding multiple-choice item is a crucial problem for all further study of Piagetian problems using multiple-choice items. After careful examination of the IEA tests parallel with extensive perusal of the Piagetian literature the item IEA/1A:16 was found to have close correspondence with the experiment "Equilibrium in the Balance" (Inhelder and Piaget, 1958, pp. 165–181).

The next problem was to make the qualitative evidence derived from the Piagetian experiment comparable with the quantitative data that could be attained from the IEA item. At this point the accuracy and validity of prediction from the reported evidence to the IEA item was questioned.

By regarding each distractor in the IEA item as a member of the set of all possible answers to the problem studied in the Piagetian experiment, the qualitative analysis of individual answers could be extended to classification of the distractors on the hypothetical stages of thinking. This was done under the unprobed presupposition that an individual's choice of distractor would be that which most closely resembled the one that he himself could spontaneously produce. The classification of distractors on a scale of stages of thinking made it possible to test the validity of the Piagetian theory by specifying hypotheses about expected behavior in the IEA item of individuals classified on stages of thinking according to their choice of distractor.

2. Method

a. Subjects

The subjects included in the analysis of the item IEA/1A:16 were 823 Swedish boys, 747 Swedish girls, and 736 Indian boys. Those missing on this particular item as well as the "illiterates" and "different thinking" groups were eliminated prior to the analysis. Subjects were the same as in the whole study (See page 18).

b. Apparatus

The two types of balance scales used by Piaget are shown in figure 3.1.

Inhelder and Piaget (1958, p. 164) described the problem of the study:

> The experiment was set up in a way that would force the question of proportionality. When two equal weights W and W' are balanced at unequal distances from an axis L and L', the amounts of work WH and W'H' needed to move to the heights H and H' corresponding to these distances are equal. Thus, we have the double (inverse) proportion:
>
> $$W/W' = L'/L = H'/H$$
>
> The result is that finding the law presupposes the construction of the proportion $W/W' = L'/L$ and spelling out its explanation implies an understanding of the proportion $W/W' = H'/H$. It seemed to us that it would be interesting to study how this proportionality schema develops as it is linked with the equilibrium schema.

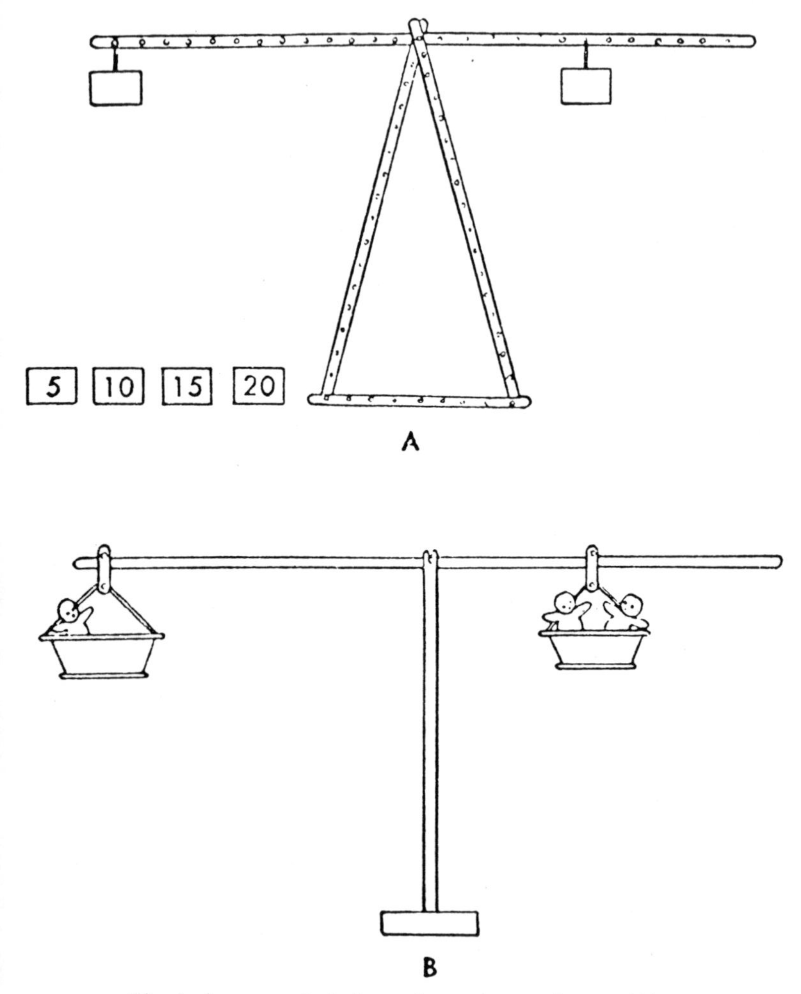

The balance scale is here shown in two forms: (A) a conventional balance with varying weights which can be hung at different points along the crossbar; (B) a balance equipped with baskets which can be moved along the crossbar to different points and in which dolls are used as weights.

Figure 3.1 *The Balance Scales used by Jean Piaget*

The same problem could be studied by using the corresponding four pictures of different balance scales, shown in item IEA/1A:16. (Appendix I).

There are two major differences between the Piagetian experiment and item IEA/1A:16:(a). The variables–both weight (W and W') and distance (L and L')–can assume more than two values in the experiment, but only two in the item; and (b). The third variable in the experiment, H, is a constant in the item.

These differences probably affect the difficulty level of the problem, making the IEA item easier than the experiment, but not the logic of the problem.

c. Theory-oriented Item Analysis

The analysis of item IEA/1A:16 may not be regarded as just a replication study using different stimuli. Since Piaget has extended his analysis of the experiment "Equilibirum in the Balance" into the development of his logical model–the present study can use his model for two purposes, both for description of the distractors and for validation of hypotheses based on the theory.

The logical description of distractors A–D and classifications of them are presented in Table 3.6.

Table 3.6. *Theory-oriented Item Analysis, item IEA/1A:16*

Distractor	Logical description	Classification
A	$W/W' = L/L$	Pre-operational thinking
B	$W'/W = L'/L'$	Pre-operational thinking
C	$W/W' = L/L'$	Concrete operational thinking
D	$W'/W = L'/L$	Formal operational thinking

Where: W = 100 pounds
W' = 50 pounds
L = distance from the axis equals half the balance
L' = distance from the axis equals a quarter of the balance

d. Hypothesis

If the developmental sequence progresses from pre-operational thinking into concrete operational thinking and on to formal operational thinking, there will be significant successive increases in performance on verbal intelligence tests (Word Knowledge, IEA/2F; Reading Comprehension, IEA/3C, 3D) as well as in school achievement (Science I, IEA/1A, 1B) between groups classified on three stages of thinking.

e. Method of Analysis
Analysis of variance, one-way classification, was carried through for testing the significance of the difference between three group means. Separate analyses were carried through on three dependent variables: Word Knowledge, Reading Comprehension, Science I.

There are three basic assumptions underlying the analysis of variance: (a) that the distribution of the variables in the population from which the samples are drawn are normal; (b) that the variances are equal in the population from which the samples are drawn, i.e., the assumption of homogeneity of variance; and (c) that the effects of various factors on the total variation are additive (Ferguson, 1966, p. 294).

The kurtosis and skewness of the three criterion variables were inspected in order to control the assumption of normal distribution in the variables. (See Table 3.7). None of them exactly corresponds to the normal distribution. As pointed out by Ferguson (*ibid.*) it is probable that the conclusions drawn from the data using an F test will not be seriously affected unless there are fairly extreme departure from normality.

Table 3.7. *Kurtosis and Skewness of Three Variables*

	Reading comprehension		Word knowledge		Science total	
	Kurtosis	Skewness	Kurtosis	Skewness	Kurtosis	Skewness
Sweden, boys	–.943	–.229	.392	–.473	–.347	–.060
Sweden, girls	–.456	–.406	.719	–.421	–.176	–.241
India, boys	–.671	.443	–.715	.106	–.508	.064

Homogeneity of variances of groups, classified on the basis of choice of distractor in item IEA/1A:16, was tested by the method developed by Cochran (Winer, 1970, p. 94).

Table 3.8. *Test of Homogeneity of Variance of item IEA/1A:16*

	Reading comprehension		Word knowledge		Science total	
	Cochran C	p	Cochran C	p	Cochran C	p
Sweden, boys	.348	NS	.357	NS	.370	NS
Sweden, girls	.377	NS	.427	NS	.392	$<.05$
India, boys	.455	$<.001$	.409	$<.01$	.500	$<.001$

As seen in Table 3.8 the homogeneity of variance of verbal intelligence tests (Word Knowledge, Reading Comprehension) was non-significant for Swedish boys and girls. It was also non-significant for Swedish boys in the Science test (Science I). The basic assumption is verified for these tests and groups.

Departure from homogeneity is seen on all three tests on the Indian sample as well as for Swedish girls in the Science test. As Winer has pointed out, the experimenter need only be concerned about relatively large departures from the hypothesis of equal population variances, because F tests are robust with respect to departures from homogeneity of variance (Winer, *ibid*, pp. 92–93).

The assumption about additivity was not tested as there was no basis for doubt about its validity.

The deviations from basic assumptions will call for cautiousness in the interpretation of tests of significance.

3. Result

a. A Summary of the Data

Table 3.9 summarizes the results achieved by Swedish boys, Swedish girls and Indian boys classified on three stages of thinking according to their choice of distractor in item IEA/1A:16, on two verbal intelligence tests (Reading Comprehension, Word Knowledge) and on a test of school performance in Science (Science I).

Table 3.9. ***Means and Standard Deviations for Groups Classified on the Basis of Choice of Distractor in Item IEA/1A:16***

			Criterion variables					
			Reading comprehension		Word knowledge		Science	
Sample	Distractor	N	$\bar{X}$	s	$\bar{X}$	s	$\bar{X}$	s
Sweden, boys	A,B	71	15.93	10.08	10.54	8.13	13.35	5.98
	C	102	19.26	10.36	13.27	8.00	17.21	6.83
	D	650	23.28	9.98	15.72	7.44	21.26	6.61
Sweden, girls	A,B	78	19.86	9.79	11.76	8.53	13.34	6.95
	C	160	21.50	9.14	14.24	7.15	16.00	6.27
	D	509	24.16	8.65	14.88	6.82	19.50	5.97
India, boys	A,B	207	10.15	6.27	10.85	8.89	6.74	6.12
	C	137	12.02	7.64	16.33	11.34	10.12	8.65
	D	392	15.00	9.03	18.11	10.35	13.48	6.12

b. Tests of Significance

Table 3.10 summarizes tests of significance carried through by analysis of variance, one-way classification. A full report of the significance testing is presented in Appendix II.

Table 3.10. ***Summary of F tests for Groups Classified on Basis of Choice of Distractor in Item IEA/1A:16***

	Criterion variables		
	Reading comprehension	Word knowledge	Science
Sweden, boys	F = 22.02 ***	F = 17.90 ***	F = 57.08 ***
Sweden, girls	F = 11.38 ***	F = 6.62 **	F = 46.09 ***
India, boys	F = 25.81 ***	F = 34.95 ***	F = 70.81 ***

** $p < .01$ *** $p < .001$

The hypothesis was confirmed for all three criteria in the three samples, Swedish boys, Swedish girls and Indian boys.

4. Implications

The finding, that individuals on three different stages of thinking differ significantly in performance on verbal intelligence tests (Word Knowledge, IEA/2F; Reading Comprehension, IEA/3C, 3D) as well as in school achievement in Science (Science I, IEA/1A, 1B) ,has the following implications:

1. Piagetian problems can be studied by using multiple-choice items;
2. The logical model advanced by Piaget can be used for theory-oriented item analysis in order to set up hypotheses about expected behavior at different stages of thinking; and
3. The findings of Piaget in the experiment "Equilibrium in the Balance" are confirmed on the basis of the item IEA/1A:16.

E. ITEM ANALYSES

Seven items were chosen for this study—IEA/1A:8, 1A:9, 1A:10, 1A:14, 1A:16, 1A:20, 1B:10. Three types of item analyses were conducted with them:

1. a study of the difficulty and the discriminating power of the items;
2. a criterion-related analysis;
3. a theory-oriented analysis.

1. Difficulty and Discriminating Power

Item analysis usually reports two values relating to level of difficulty and index of discrimination respectively. Difficulty is defined as the percentage of the respondents who gave the right answer. Index of discrimination is reported as the power of the item to discriminate between students with high scores and students with low scores on the test using the point biserial correlation (r_{pbis}).

Table 3.11 gives the difficulty value and index of discrimination for Sweden and India, based on the total samples of the IEA study and not on the restricted sample employed in this study.

Table 3.11. *Difficulty Value (p) and Index of Discrimination (r_{pbis}) of Seven Items, Sweden and India, Total Samples* [a]

Item nr	Sweden		India	
	p	r_{pbis}	p	r_{pbis}
IEA/1A:8	.474	.378	.272	.210
IEA/1A:9	.389	.392	.344	.426
IEA/1A:10	.707	.348	.560	.554
IEA/1A:14	.651	.303	.311	.262
IEA/1A:16	.640	.386	.351	.379
IEA/1A:20	.495	.473	.243	.364
IEA/1B:10	.411	.339	.321	.414.

[a]Sweden, sum of weights = 2041; India, sum of weights = 2731

2. Criterion-related Item Analysis

The study of difficulty and discriminating power of items takes into consideration only the right/wrong dichotomy as it is related to performance in the total test. New measures are needed, for several reasons, when multiple-choice items with one right and four wrong alternatives are changed into a scale ignoring the right/wrong dichotomy in favor of assigning the distractors to three hypothetical stages of thinking. First, the use of an internal criterion in the point biserial correlation (total test score) has to be questioned. When the items are used for testing something other than the total test from which they were taken, new external criteria have to be chosen for the study of discriminating power. Secondly, given a good external criterion a test of significance of the differences between the means of the groups who have chosen the various distractors can be used for investigating (a) if distractors classified as measuring the same stage of thinking are not significantly different from each other in the criterion variable, (b) if distractors classified as measuring different stages of thinking are significantly different from each other with the difference in the expected direction.

Piaget describes a type of intelligence for which no suitable external criterion could be found in the IEA test battery. The two verbal intelligence tests, the Word Knowledge test (IEA/2F) and the Reading Comprehension test (IEA/3C, 3D) were the closest approximations available to a measure of this type of intelligence.

Criterion-related item analysis data of the seven items using these two intelligence tests as criteria are reported in Appendix III (Tables 1–14).

3. Theory-oriented Item Analysis

a. Introduction

The fundamental idea of any deductive theory is that it should be possible to condense all information available in a specific field into a few components which can be stated in a language as precise as that of mathematics. Jean Piaget has tried to use the language of logic in building his logical model of the development of thinking.

The second phase of theory-building is that of confirmation or validation, which is accomplished by induction. If the theory is valid the predictions from its postulates must be confirmed.

The type of theory-oriented item analysis used in this study represents an attempt to use the language of the theory to describe the ways of thinking hypothesized to cause the choice of distractors in some multiple-choice items.

The basis for the validation phase was the assignment of item distractors to different stages of thinking, making possible the advancement of hypotheses about different levels of performance in some particular criterion variable by individuals classified according to their choice of distractor.

In the following pages the development and use of the method labelled *theory-oriented item analysis* (TOI) will be spelled out.

1. The method was "invented" and successfully employed on item IEA/1A:16, as reported earlier in the present study (pp. 20 ff.).
2. A number of consequences are implicit in the method:
   a. The method has important consequences for the design of the present study;
   b. The method solves a linguistic problem in that it provides a technical language appropriate for description of the process of thinking, isolated from the objects of thinking;
   c. The method is best suited for analyses of items testing effects of environmental stimulation in general elementary learning—but the possible effects of specific instruction in school must also be considered.
3. The method will be described in terms of the steps taken in analysis of any item in the study.
4. Finally, the results in terms of classifications of distactors on stages of thinking will be reported.

As there was no sufficiently good criterion variable in the IEA battery of instruments for testing the reliability of the classifications, a separate study of this was undertaken on the two lower stages of thinking (pre-operational and concrete operational thinking). This study will be reported at the end of this section.

b. A Method for the Study of Validity of the Piagetian Theory

The development of the method labelled theory-oriented item analysis (TOI) was closely related to the problem of whether the Piagetian theory can be applied to areas not yet investigated.

It was necessary to develop this method in order to make it possible to use items that had no direct correspondence to Piagetian experiments but in which the choice of distractor might be hypothesized to be related to the type of thinking described by Piaget.

As shown on page 23, it was possible to use the logical model for theory-oriented item analysis of item IEA/1A:16 in order to formulate hypotheses about expected behavior at different stages of thinking.

This important finding encouraged us to try to standardize the procedure, successfully adopted to item IEA/1A:16, into use on other problems. The development of the study, from an idea of correspondence between item and experiment on one particular item to a study of validity using the method of theory-oriented item analysis, is best seen in an overview of the general procedure adopted in the present research.

c. General Procedure Adopted in the Research

Figure 3.2. presents three basic models of the study, (a) first, the direct comparison between Piagetian experiment and test item, (b) then, the complete model of interpretation of items with corresponding experiment, and (c) finally, the model of induction from the theory, applying this into new problem areas.

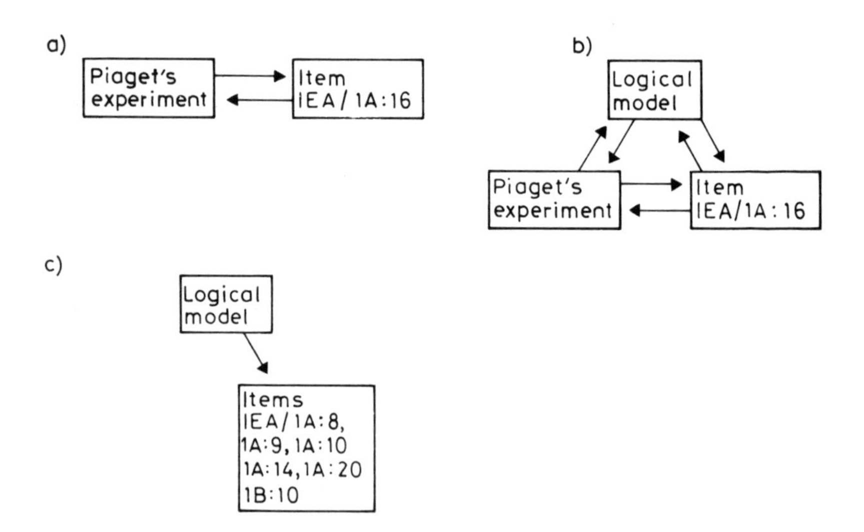

Figure 3.2. *Basic models of the Study, (a) Direct Comparision, (b) Theory-oriented Comparison and Interpretation, (c) Inductive Application of the Model on New Problems.*

The direct comparison can, as was pointed out earlier, be regarded as an introduction to the theory-oriented comparison and interpretation which attempts to use the Piagetian evidence as fully as possible in formulating hypotheses about children's behavior when faced with the problem of item IEA/1A:16.

The final step, induction from the theory into new problem areas, can be regarded as the step into the study of the validity of the theory.

d. The Language Problem of the TOI

There are two fundamental problems of the TOI:

1. how to abstract the mode of thinking involved in solving multiple-choice items from the content of the items?
2. how to describe the mode of thinking hypothesized in such a way that items related to not yet investigated problems can be studied?

In his later studies Piaget himself has solved the problem of finding a language that made it possible to describe the development of thinking isolated from the content of the problem under investigation, by introducing the language of logic into the field of psychology.

For the present study this language opened up the possibility of describing the modes of thinking hypothesized to cause the choice of distractors in multiple-choice items, introducing Piaget's logic into the rationale of the TOI. For an introduction to Piaget's logic, see Mays (1956).

e. Opportunity to learn

It should be noted both with regard to the construction of the Science test (IEA/1A, 1B) and the interpretation of the results that, in spite of the interest in studying the opportunity to learn the content area of each item, the general comment about the test advanced by the principal investigators (Comber and Keeves, 1973, p. 33) was that

> "Most of the knowledge and understanding tested at this stage is not likely to be the result of specific Science teaching but of reciprocity to opportunities provided by the environment in general elementary learning situations."

f. The Method

The TOI was conducted in six steps:

1. Description of the problem,
2. Isolation of the variables in the problem,
3. Determination of the values on these variables,
4. Description of the problem in terms of the Piagetian logic,
5. Classification of the distractors on the developmental stages of the Piagetian theory, and
6. Specification of hypotheses to be tested.

g. Theory-oriented Item Analysis of Seven IEA Items

A summary of the theory-oriented item analysis of seven IEA-items is given in Table 3.12.

Table 3.12. ***Summary of Theory-oriented Item Analysis of seven IEA items***

Item nr	Stages of thinking		
	Pre-operational thinking	Concrete operational thinking	Formal operational thinking
IEA/1A:8	A, E	C, D	B
IEA/1A:9	D, E	A, C	B
IEA/1A:10	A, E	B, C	D
IEA/1A:14	E	B, C, D	A
IEA/1A:16	A, B	C	D
IEA/1A:20	B, C, E	A	D
IEA/1B:10	A, C	D, E	B

4. Reliability of Classifications of Distractors

A separate study of the accuracy of the classifications of distractors on stages of thinking was regarded necessary for three reasons:

1. The validity of the Piagetian theory cannot be tested unless the classifications are correct; misclassifications will lead to a false impression of low validity, even if the theory is valid.
2. The validity of the test instruments that will be constructed in order to test the development of thinking in terms of the Piagetian theory will be seriously affected if the classifications are incorrect to a considerable extent.
3. The results of criterion-related item analysis, reported above, using the Word Knowledge test (IEA/2F) as a criterion, were somewhat inconsistent with an analysis using the Reading Comprehension test (IEA/3C, 3D) as a criterion, thus throwing some doubt upon the usefulness of these tests as criteria in studies of the type of intelligence described by Piaget.

The classification to be checked is chiefly the separation of distractors normally classified as "wrongs" into the two groups: "pre-operational thinking" and "concrete operational thinking." The classification "formal operational thinking" is in these items always connected with the usual classification "right."

The hypothesis to be tested was that the "wrongs" in the group of seven multiple-choice items are scalable using scalogram analysis if and only if both (1) there is such a thing as distinct stages of thinking, and (2) there are no misclassifications.

The group of students best suited for a test of this hypothesis was composed of individuals who were not classified as "illiterates" but who nonetheless had chosen only "wrongs" on the group of items under investigation.

Study of Reliability of Classifications of Distractors

The importance of a study of the reliability of the classifications of distractors on various stages of thinking can be conceived of in two ways:

1. As the final control of the theory-oriented item analysis that had taken the step of induction from the logical model into hypotheses about expected behavior in new problem areas.
2. As the starting point of the test construction if the results did confirm the hypothesis that there are distinct stages of thinking into which the distractors can be reliably classified.

Problem: to assess the reliability of the classifications of item distractors made in the theory-oriented item analysis.

Hypothesis: the items will be scalable using scalogram analysis if the classifications are sufficiently accurate.

Subjects: the low-achieving subjects chosen for this analysis had two characteristics:

1. They had not answered correctly any item in the group of three items under investigation in each analysis,
2. They were not classified as "illiterates" or "different thinking."

Analysis 1: Subjects with no correct answer in items IEA/1A:9, 1A:16 and 1B:10 were 66 Swedish boys, 88 Swedish girls and 157 Indian boys.

Analysis 2: Subjects with no correct answer in items IEA/1A:10, 1A:14 and 1A:16 were 20 Swedish boys, 30 Swedish girls and 110 Indian boys.

Analysis 3: Subjects with no correct answer in items IEA/1A:8, 1A:16 and 1A:20 were 60 Swedish boys, 81 Swedish girls and 167 Indian boys.

It was assumed that these groups would contain not only low-achieving subjects but also some with low motivation as well. Low-achievers with good motivation were expected to answer according to their level of maturity, but those with low motivation would tend to do more random guessing, which would affect the scalability and produce coefficients that were lower than the "true" values.

Method of Analysis
Scalogram analysis was carried through using only one cutting-point on any item, making distractors classified as pre-operational thinking into zeros and distractors classified as concrete operational thinking into ones.

The Guttman scales constructed in the three analyses were:
Analysis 1: GUTSCIC = 1A:9(2), 1A:16(2), 1B:10(2);
Analysis 2: GUTSC2D = 1A:10(2), 1A:14(2), 1A:16(2);
Analysis 3: GUTSC3A = 1A:8(2), 1A:16(2), 1A:20(2).

Result
Appendix IV, Tables 1 and 2 summarize the scale types and the coefficients obtained for Swedish boys, Swedish girls, Swedish total, and Indian boys.

Keeping in mind the group of students with low motivation, the coefficients obtained give strong evidence for the empirical basis of classifications on two levels of performance, which were described as pre-operational thinking and concrete operational thinking.

Implications
The classifications of distractors on stages of thinking were regarded as reliable enough to justify further test construction and use in the study.

F. TEST INSTRUMENTS II: GUTTMAN SCALES BASED ON SEVEN IEA ITEMS

1. Introduction

a. The Search for Structure of Answering Patterns

Seven multiple-choice items with five distractors each offer a large number of possible response patterns. Any hypothesis of structure implies a reduction of the number of patterns. On the other hand, lack of structure would result in a random selection of distractors, except for a preference for the "right" answer.

A series of attempts were made to reveal the response patterns. First, all patterns in the data were listed and the frequencies of the different patterns were summed, which gave some support for the hypothesis of some structure in the data. Secondly, different factor analytical approaches were tried, but the factor analysis failed as the dummy-variables constructed out of a certain item were nested, and the items were rearranged as factors.

The type of structure we tried to establish was the unidimensional cumulative development from answers based on pre-operational thinking, on to answers based on concrete operational thinking and finally to answers based on formal operational thinking. Scalogram analysis is a method which makes it possible to test hypothetical structures of this type.

b. Scalogram analysis

The hypothesis tested by means of a scalogram analysis is that an almost perfect relationship exists among items. This relationship is given by the definition of a scale: a perfect scale is one in which a person who passes an item of given difficulty will also pass any other item of lesser difficulty; and an individual who fails an item of given difficulty will also fail any other item of greater difficulty. Guttman's definition (1950, p. 62) reads as follows:

> "We shall call a set of items of common content a scale if a person with a higher rank than another person is just as high or higher on every item than the other person."

The aims of scalogram analysis as used in the present study are twofold: first, to determine the empirical basis for the hypothesis that a set of items can be logically ordered on a scale in terms of a given property described of the items; secondly, to determine whether the subjects, when they respond to the items, can be ordered on a scale in terms of the given property of the items.

These contradictory aims of scalogram analysis could be used in the present study because it started in the logical model, stating specific hypotheses to be tested: Hypotheses 1 and 2 as well as the hypothesis of page 33 are related to the first aim, and Hypotheses 3–6 are related to the second.

The Guttman model can be used both in dichotomous items and in those having more than two response categories. It is the boundary between response categories which is considered to be located on the scale. One trichotomous item is formally equivalent to two dichotomous items, except for the fact that a respondent selects only one category, no matter how many are offered.

What is essential is the ordering of response categories in an ordered sequence from highest to lowest. For the present study this ordering was based entirely on the theory-oriented item analysis, giving responses classified as formal operational thinking the score of 3, concrete operational thinking the score of 2 and pre-operational thinking the score of 1.

Scaling the IEA items this way gives three scores to any item and, consequently, two possible cutting-points for the scalogram analysis: (2) read as "passes" equal to responses based on concrete or formal operational thinking and "fails" based on pre-operational thinking, and (3) read as "passes" equal to responses based on formal operational thinking and "fails" based on pre-operational or concrete operational thinking.

The criteria used in making the decision whether a table of data conforms to the scale hypothesis are functional unity criteria, which refer to a particular type of consistency to be observed within the data.

All scalogram analyses were computed by using a computer program for Guttman scaling, originally developed by Anderson (1966), modified by Anderson and Ofshe to handle multiple cutting points, and finally adapted to the system of computer programs SPSS under the name of Subprogram Guttman Scale (Nie, Bent and Hull, 1970, pp. 196–207).

2. Scale Construction—Ten Guttman Scales

Ten Guttman scales were constructed both for Indian boys and for Swedish boys and girls. A scale was accepted as successful if it gave a coefficient of reproducibility of $> .80$. The optimal coefficient of reproducibility to be looked for, i.e., $> .90$, was obtained for one scale, GUTSC2A, with Indian boys.

Two scales were constructed using items IEA/1A:9, 1A:16, 1B:10:

GUTSC1A = 1A:9(2), 1A:16(2), 1B:10(3)

GUTSC1B = 1A:9(3), 1A:16(2), 1B:10(3)

Division points are given in brackets.

Four scales were constructed using items IEA/1A:10, 1A:14, 1A:16:

GUTSC2A = 1A:10(2), 1A:14(3), 1A:16(2)
GUTSC2B = 1A:10(3), 1A:14(3), 1A:16(2)
GUTSC2C = 1A:10(2), 1A:14(3), 1A:16(3)
GUTSC2E = 1A:10(2), 1A:14(2), 1A:16(3)

Finally, four scales were constructed using items IEA/1A:8, 1A:16, 1A:20:

GUTSC3A = 1A:8(2), 1A:16(2), 1A:20(2)
GUTSC3B = 1A:8(3), 1A:16(2), 1A:20(2)
GUTSC3C = 1A:8(2), 1A:16(2), 1A:20(3)
GUTSC3D = 1A:8(3), 1A:16(2), 1A:20(3)

Scale types and coefficients for the ten Guttman scales appear in Appendix V.

3. Reliability of Guttman Scales

In a discussion of the problems of reliabiltiy of Guttman scales, Guttman (1950, pp. 277–311) shows that scalogram analysis provides as an automatic biproduct the assurance that responses to individual items and total scores both have relatively little error of measurement if the reproducibility is high (i.e., coefficient of reproducibility $\geqslant .90$). He suggests that the sampling theory of ordinary proportions can be used as an approximation to the sampling theory of the coefficient of reproducibility. From this it follows that the sampling variance follows the coefficient of reproducibility, so that when the coefficient of reproducibility is high the sampling variance will be small and the reliability estimate high.

Guttman has pointed out that the Spearman Brown prophesy formula cannot be used on Guttman scales because the assumptions behind such a formula cannot be fulfilled. He also showed that the split-half reliability is very sensitive to differences in the marginal frequencies. Thus, the best estimate of the reliability of Guttman scales is the coefficient of reproducibility. A still better estimate is provided by using the three newer coefficients, the minimum marginal reproducibility, the percent improvement, and the coefficient of scalability.

a. Study of Reliability through Comparison between Subgroups

Reliability is by definition the tendency towards consistency from one set of measurements to another. Unreliability on the other hand, is the fact that repeated sets of measurements tend not to duplicate one another but to show a certain spread (Ekman, 1947).

Since the present investigation was a pilot study for future survey-studies of the development of logical thinking it was of pivotal importance to see if the instruments were reliable enough to allow comparisons between subgroups in the sample.

The reasons for using pre-defined subgroups instead of random split were:

a. Guttman's discarding of the split-half reliability as not applicable to his scales; and
b. the wish to make possible inspection of changes from one subgroups to another, and to test the degree of significance of differences between these subgroups.

Three Guttman scales were chosen for this study of reliability, GUTSC1B, GUTSC2B, GUTSC3D. All other Guttman scales constructed were so highly correlated with one of these, that they could represent the other scales as well. (See Appendix VI, tables 1 to 3).

In assessing the reliability of the three Guttman scales, it was of interest to compare differences across category boundaries for subgroups, characterized by culture (Sweden, India), sex (Swedish boys and girls), age (10:0–10:5, 10:6–10:11) and SES[2] (Sweden: high, medium, low). Data used in the comparisons are in the form of Guttman scale parameters. Each Guttman scale has three category boundaries which separate the four levels in the development of thinking scheme. The category boundary is given as a standard score to indicate what part of the normal distribution is on or below a certain level of thinking. The Guttman scale parameters have been calculated on the above mentioned subgroups.

[2] The classification in three socio-economic status levels was based on student's report of father's occupation, coded into nine categories representing main classes in the occupational hierarchy. (See Husén, *et al.*, 1973, pp. 100–103; Huséen, 1967, I, pp. 139–146). SES high equals categories nine and eight; SES medium equals categories seven to three; SES low equals categories two, one and unclassified.

Table 3.13. *Category Boundaries for three Guttman Scales (GUTSC1B, GUTSC2B, GUTSC3D) by Culture, Sex and Age*

Scale	Age[a]	Sweden, boys 1	Sweden, boys 2	Sweden, girls 1	Sweden, girls 2	India, boys 1	India, boys 2
GUTSC1B	0	−1.64	−2.00	−1.55	−1.70	−1.13	− .96
	1	− .19	− .41	− .23	− .41	− .05	− .07
	2	1.08	.87	.93	.77	1.17	.95
GUTSC2B	0	−1.93	−2.33	−1.94	−2.39	−1.31	−1.15
	1	−1.07	−1.29	− .88	−1.15	− .50	− .33
	2	.04	− .16	.34	.18	.64	.86
GUTSC3D	0	−1.66	−1.92	−1.51	−1.78	−1.16	− .93
	1	− .43	− .85	− .39	− .69	.16	.48
	2	.71	.24	.78	.60	1.57	1.58

[a] Age 1 = 10:0–10:5, Age 2 = 10:6–10:11

Table 3.14. *Category Boundaries for three Guttman Scales (GUTSC1B, GUTSC2B, GUTSC3D) by Culture, Sex and Grade*

Scale	Grade	Sweden, boys 3	Sweden, boys 4	Sweden, girls 3	Sweden, girls 4
GUTSC1B	0	−1.65	−1.95	−1.58	−1.67
	1	− .12	− .46	− .19	− .42
	2	1.14	.84	1.06	.71
GUTSC2B	0	−1.90	−2.36	−1.92	−2.34
	1	−1.05	−1.30	− .87	−1.12
	2	.09	− .19	.39	.16
GUTSC3D	0	−1.67	−1.88	−1.51	−1.75
	1	− .40	− .86	− .43	− .61
	2	.74	.24	.80	.61

Scale	Grade	India, boys 3	India, boys 4	India, boys 5	India, boys 6
GUTSC1B	0	−1.21	−1.07	− .96	− .98
	1	.09	.00	.01	− .06
	2	1.20	1.13	1.09	.60
GUTSC2B	0	−1.25	−1.10	−1.27	−1.46
	1	− .44	− .46	− .37	− .39
	2	.70	.64	.84	.83
GUTSC3D	0	−1.10	−1.11	− .97	− .93
	1	.51	.27	.36	− .02
	2	1.56	1.57	1.67	1.35

Table 3.15. *Category Boundaries for Three Guttman Scales (GUTSC1B, GUTSC2B, GUTSC3D) by Sex and SES and Age, Sweden*

		Sweden, boys					
SES		High		Medium		Low	
Age		1	2	1	2	1	2
Scale							
GUTSC1B	0	–	–	−1.63	−2.31	−1.51	−1.68
	1	− .35	−1.10	− .23	− .36	− .08	− .39
	2	.87	.35	.95	1.02	1.38	.90
GUTSC2B	0	−1.73	–	−2.17	−2.32	−1.78	−2.24
	1	−1.38	−1.59	−1.09	−1.27	− .98	−1.24
	2	.05	− .64	.10	− .19	− .05	.02
GUTSC3D	0	−2.04	–	−1.59	−1.94	−1.66	−1.77
	1	− .74	−2.07	− .47	− .84	− .28	− .66
	2	.37	− .24	.73	.23	.81	.41

		Sweden, girls					
SES		High		Medium		Low	
Age		1	2	1	2	1	2
Scale							
GUTSC1B	0	−1.49	−2.05	−1.97	−1.69	−1.28	−1.65
	1	− .66	− .52	− .19	− .43	− .09	− .33
	2	.56	.71	.90	.88	1.21	.66
GUTSC2B	0	−2.15	–	−2.11	−2.30	−1.73	−2.40
	1	−1.42	−1.17	− .94	−1.10	− .65	−1.21
	2	.12	.00	.30	.26	.44	.15
GUTSC3D	0	−1.26	−2.05	−1.79	−1.70	−1.39	−1.84
	1	− .40	− .98	− .50	− .65	− .24	− .63
	2	.40	.28	.83	.65	.92	.66

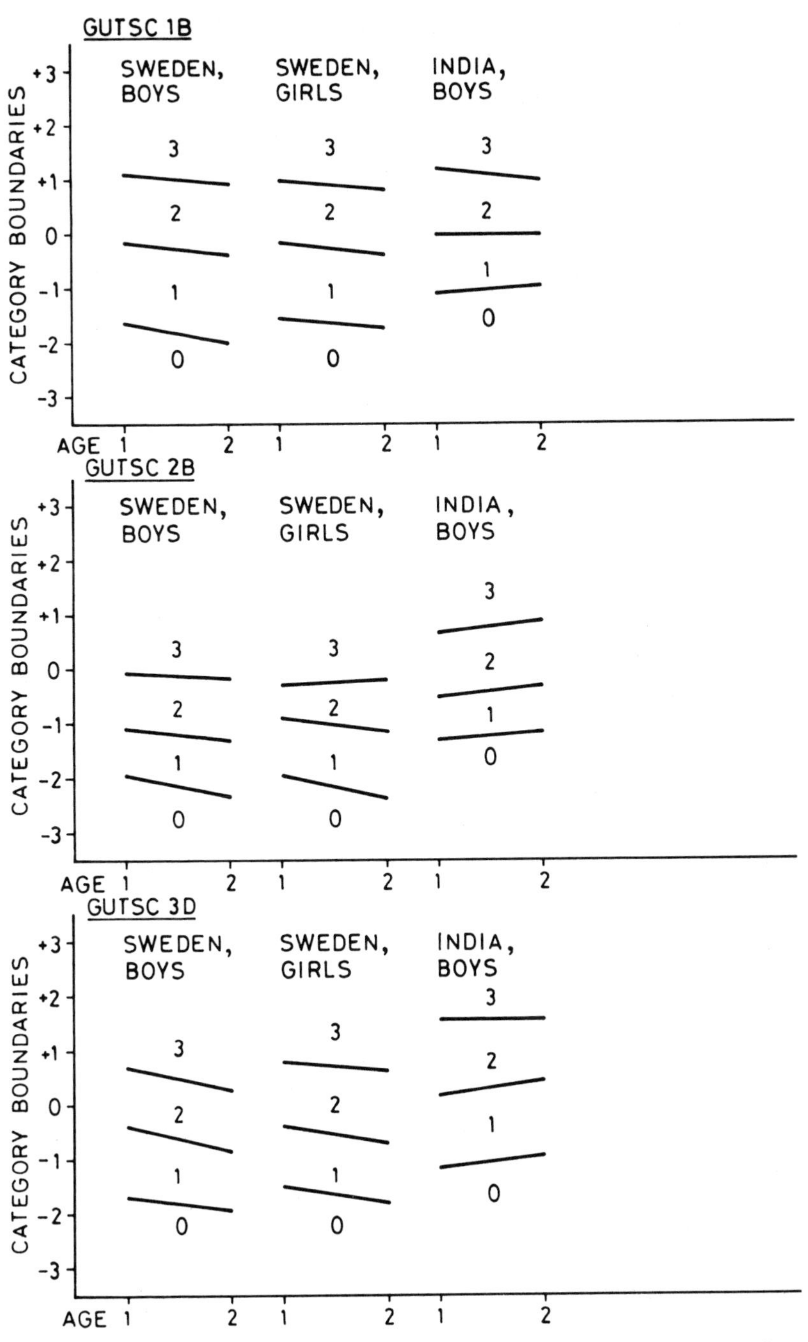

Figure 3.3. *Category Boundaries for three Guttman scales (GUTSC1B, GUTSC2B, GUTSC3D) by culture, sex and age (1 = 10:0–10:5, 2 = 10:6–10:11).*

Three sources of variation (age, grade in school, social background) might be expected to affect all scales in a similar way: a consistent movement towards higher levels of thinking as the child grows older, is exposed to more schooling and receives the richer environmental stimulation associated with social background characteristics.

As seen in Figure 3.3, age differences for Swedish boys and girls go in the expected direction on all scales. But the Indian boys behave more inconsistently, probably as a consequence of interaction of age x social background x grade in school.

As seen in Figure 3.4, differences between groups with different numbers of years in school go in the expected direction for Swedish boys and girls. In fact, age and grade in school as sources of variation are practically inseparable in Sweden. The Indian boys behave more irregularly.

As seen in Figure 3.5, social background differences for Swedish boys go in the expected direction. For Swedish girls some irregularities are apparent, which might to some extent be explained by the fact that more girls than boys were classified as "different thinking."

b. Test of Significance of Differences among Category Boundaries for Subgroups

A more stringent way of making the comparisons between subgroups would be to concentrate on significant differences between scales for subgroups in the sample, and between scale levels. For each of the three Guttman scales (GUTSC1B, GUTSC2B, GUTSC3D) 204 tests of significance (51 for whole scales and 153 for scale levels) were calculated in order to make possible comparisons between the scales with regard to their sensitivity when affected by different sources of variation. The method used in these tests of significance was that employed by Lieberman (1971). A full report of age-, sex and social background differences in the development of thinking in 10-year-olds will be published separately, including also a discussion of problems of mass significance testing. For the present problem, i.e., the study of the reliability of three Guttman scales, we can confine ourselves to a summary of significant differences among the category boundaries.

As seen in Table 3.16, GUTSC1B is not very sensitive to sex differences but is about as sensitive as GUTSC3D to other sources of variation.

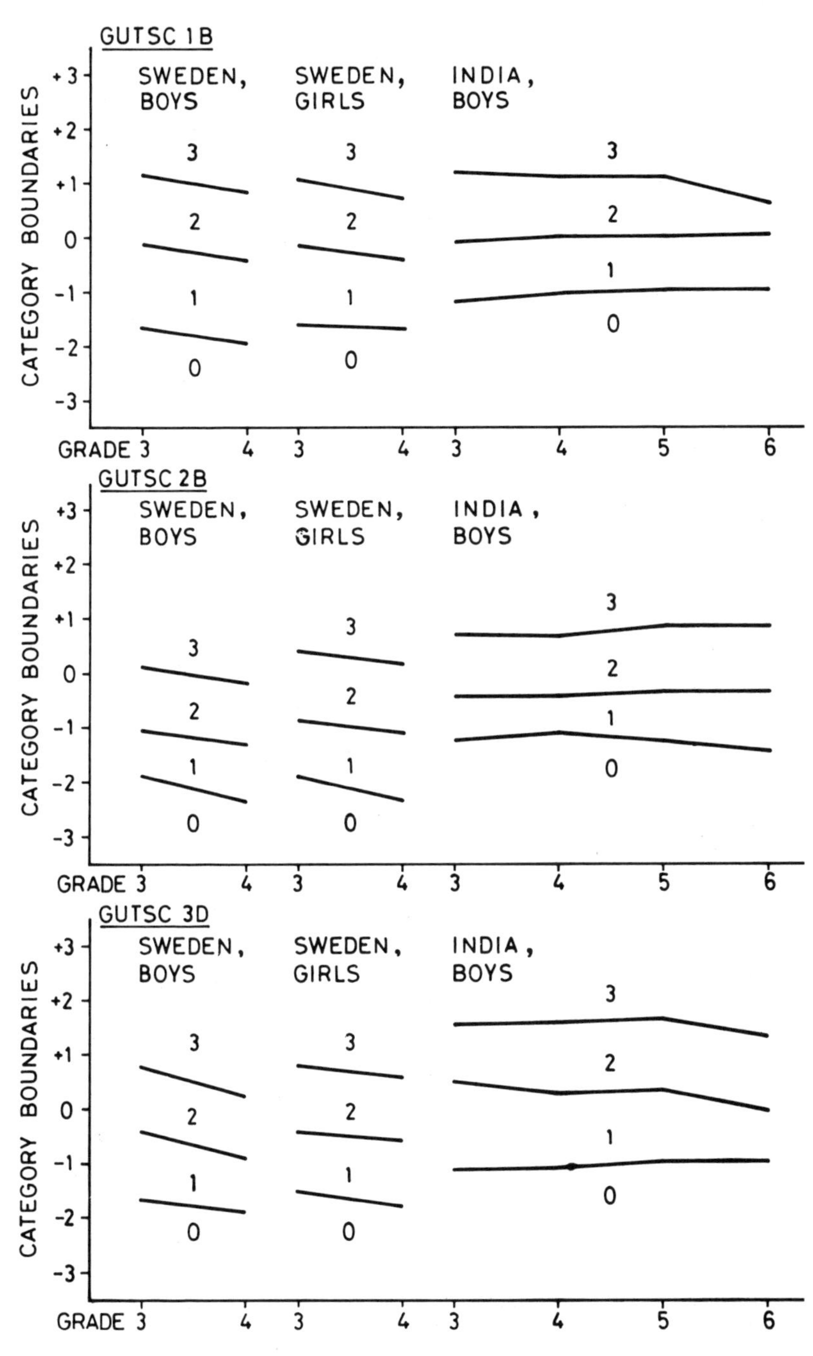

Figure 3.4. *Category Boundaries for three Guttman scales (GUTSC1B, GUTSC2B, GUTSC3D) by culture, sex and grade.*

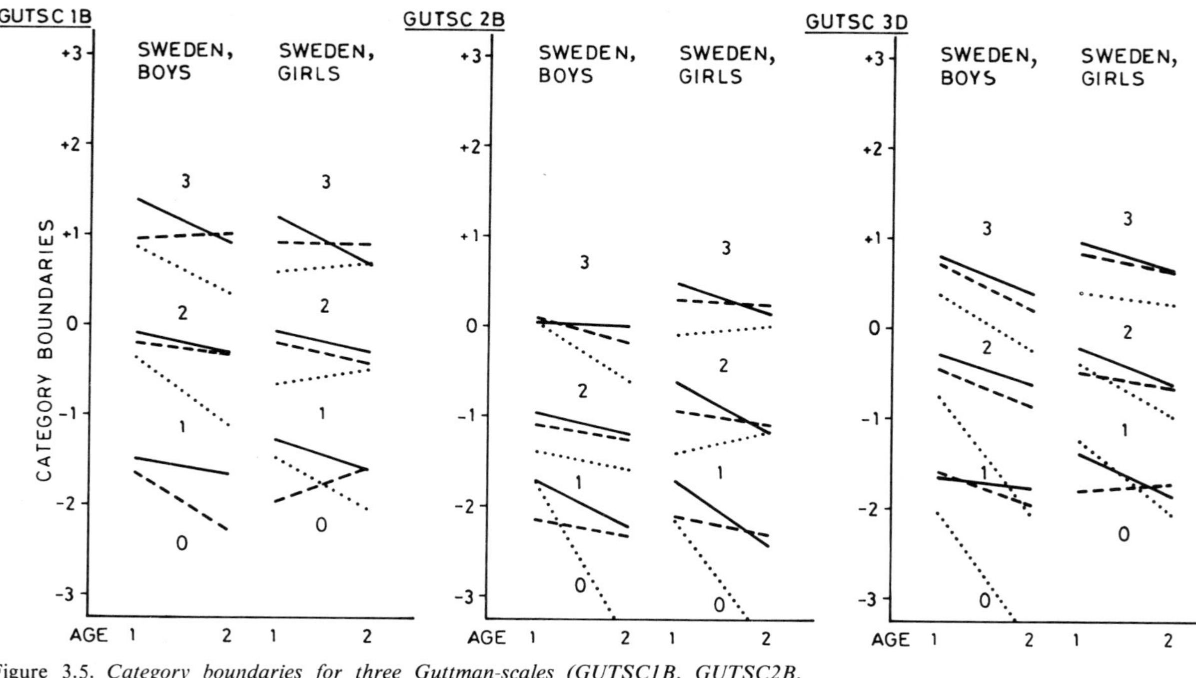

Figure 3.5. *Category boundaries for three Guttman-scales (GUTSC1B, GUTSC2B, GUTSC3D) by sex, social background and age, Sweden*

SES high · · · · · *SES medium* - - - - *SES low* ——

Table 3.16. *Summary of Significant Differences among the Category Boundaries of three Guttman Scales (GUTSC1B, GUTSC2B, GUTSC3D) for some Subgroups*

Effect studied	Subgroup		GUTSC1B	GUTSC2B	GUTSC3D
Sex effect (Sweden)	Age 1		–(–)	–(2)	–(–)
	Age 2		–(–)	–(2)	*** (2)
	Grade 3		–(–)	–(2)	–(–)
	Grade 4		–(–)	–(2)	*** (1, 2)
	SES, high		–(–)	–(–)	** (1)
	SES, medium		–(–)	–(2)	–(2)
	SES, low		–(–)	–(2)	–(–)
	SES, high,	Age 1	–(–)	–(–)	–(–)
	SES, medium,	Age 1	–(–)	–(–)	–(–)
	SES, low,	Age 1	–(–)	–(2)	–(–)
	SES, high,	Age 2	–(1)	–(–)	** (1, 2)
	SES, medium,	Age 2	–(0)	–(2)	** (2)
	SES, low,	Age 2	–(–)	–(–)	–(–)
Age effect (Sweden)	Boys		** (1)	–(–)	*** (1, 2)
	Boys, SES, high		** (1)	–(–)	*** (1, 2)
	Boys, SES, medium		–(0)	–(–)	*** (1, 2)
	Boys, SES, low		* (2)	–(–)	** (1, 2)
	Girls		–(–)	–(–)	** (1)
	Girls, SES, high		–(–)	–(–)	–(1)
	Girls, SES, medium		–(–)	–(–)	–(–)
	Girls, SES, low		** (2)	–(–)	* (1)
Grade effect (Sweden)	Boys		*** (1, 2)	–(–)	*** (1, 2)
	Girls		** (1, 2)	–(–)	* (–)
Social background effects, boys Sweden					
SES, high-medium			***(1,2)	–(–)	***(1, 2)
		Age 1	–(–)	–(–)	–(–)
		Age 2	***(1,2)	–(–)	***(1, 2)
SES, medium-low			–(–)	–(–)	–(–)
		Age 1	–(2)	–(–)	–(–)
		Age 2	–(0)	–(–)	–(–)
SES, high-low			***(1, 2)	–(–)	***(1, 2)
		Age 1	***(1, 2)	–(–)	*(1, 2)
		Age 2	***(1, 2)	–(–)	***(1, 2)
Social background effects, girls Sweden					
SES, high-medium			–(–)	–(–)	*(2)
		Age 1	*(1)	–(–)	*(2)
		Age 2	–(–)	–(–)	–(–)
SES, medium-low			–(0)	–(–)	–(–)
		Age 1	*(0)	–(–)	–(–)
		Age 2	–(–)	–(–)	–(–)
SES, high-medium			**(1)	–(–)	*(2)
		Age 1	***(1, 2)	–(–)	–(2)
		Age 2	–(–)	–(–)	–(–)

Table 3.16. *(Continued)*

Effect studied	Subgroup	GUTSC1B	GUTSC2B	GUTSC3D
India, boys				
Age effect		–(–)	–(–)	**(1)
Grade effect	Grade 3–4	–(–)	–(–)	–(–)
	Grade 4–5	–(–)	–(–)	–(–)
	Grade 5–6	–(2)	–(–)	–(1)
	Grade 3–5	–(–)	–(–)	–(–)
	Grade 3–6	*(2)	–(–)	*(1)
	Grade 4–6	*(2)	–(–)	–(–)
Social background	High-Mixed	–(–)	–(–)	–(0)
effects	Mixed-Low	–(–)	–(–)	*(2)
	High-Low	–(–)	–(–)	*(2)

Note: The significance level of the overall test for the whole scale is given in front of the brackets; within the brackets are given scale levels which differ significantly (p. $<$.05)
* p $<$.05 ** p $<$.01 *** p $<$.001

GUTSC2B is not sensitive enough to these sources of variation to show significant differences among subgroups, which probably is due to the low level of difficulty in the test items of the scale, making the variance too small and the discriminating power and/or reliability inferior to the other two scales. GUTSC3D is most sensitive to these sources of variation and is probably the most reliable scale.

G. TEST INSTRUMENTS III AND IV

1. The Thinking Test

Included in the Thinking test are 10 Guttman scales with coefficients of reproducibility > .80 in both India and Sweden.
The test score is given by the formula

$$\text{THINKING} = \frac{1}{3}\left(\frac{1}{2}\sum_{i=1}^{2} X_i + \frac{1}{4}\sum_{i=3}^{6} X_i + \frac{1}{4}\sum_{i=7}^{10} X_i\right) \tag{2}$$

where:

X_1 = GUTSC1A	X_3 = GUTSC2A	X_7 = GUTSC3A
X_2 = GUTSC1B	X_4 = GUTSC2B	X_8 = GUTSC3B
	X_5 = GUTSC2C	X_9 = GUTSC3C
	X_6 = GUTSC2E	X_{10} = GUTSC3D

Partial missing — missing in item response — that was related to one of the three groups of Guttman scales was corrected for by using one of the three alternative formulas:

$$\text{THINKING} = \frac{1}{2}\left(\frac{1}{2}\sum_{i=1}^{2} X_i + \frac{1}{4}\sum_{i=3}^{6} X_i\right) \tag{3}$$

$$\text{THINKING} = \frac{1}{2}\left(\frac{1}{2}\sum_{i=1}^{2} X_i + \frac{1}{4}\sum_{i=7}^{10} X_i\right) \tag{4}$$

$$\text{THINKING} = \frac{1}{2}\left(\frac{1}{4}\sum_{i=3}^{6} X_i + \frac{1}{4}\sum_{i=7}^{10} X_i\right) \tag{5}$$

Missing in items related to more than one of the three groups of items constituting the Guttman scales was treated as total missing.

2. The Reasoning Level Test (RL)

Seven items from the Science I test (IEA/1A, 1B) are included in the RL-test: They were recorded on a three-point scale according to the theory-oriented item analysis. Table 3.17 gives the recoding for test construction.

Table 3.17. *Recoding of Distractors of Seven Items*

Item	Preoperational thinking	Concrete operational thinking	Formal operational thinking
IEA/1A:8	A, E = 1	C, D = 2	B = 3
IEA/1A:9	D, E = 1	A, C = 2	B = 3
IEA/1A:10	A, E = 1	B, C = 2	D = 3
IEA/1A:14	E = 1	B, C, D = 2	A = 3
IEA/1A:16 *	A, B = 1	C = 2	D = 3
IEA/1A:20	B, C, E = 1	A = 2	D = 3
IEA/1B:10	A, C = 1	D, E = 2	B = 3

* E = missing

The test score was given by the formula

$$RL = \frac{1}{7} \sum_{i=1}^{7} X_i \tag{6}$$

where: X_1 to X_7 are the seven items recoded on the three-point-scale.

No correction for partial missing was used.

The RL-test has some advantages over the Thinking test:

1. The RL-test is not as sensitive to partial missing as the Thinking test, and
2. A test score on the RL-test can be more easily interpreted in relation to the Piagetian theory, for it gives the mean score of seven Piagetian tasks.

Chapter Four

Results

Hypothesis 1: A Fixed Sequence in the Development of Thinking

Hypothesis 1 predicted that the predetermined fixed sequence of stages in the development of logical thinking (pre-operational thinking, concrete operational thinking, formal operational thinking) would allow scalogram analysis.

This hypothesis can be divided into two complementary hypotheses:
(a) Pre-operational thinking would precede the two higher stages of thinking: concrete and formal operational thinking; and
(b) The two lower stages of thinking, pre-operational and concrete operational thinking, would precede the highest level of thinking: formal operational thinking.

The use of point (2) in constructing the Guttman scales corresponds to hypothesis (a) and the use of cutting point (3) corresponds to hypothesis (b). By changing the cutting points in the items used, not only can a test be performed of the scalability of different forms of the scale but also, and more important, the proposition that items with lower cutting points will always show lower relative difficulty than items with a higher cutting point can be checked with regard to its validity.

Appendix V show coefficients, score patterns and items by difficulty for ten Guttman scales. Coefficients as well as control of different forms of the scales by changing division points support Hypothesis 1.

Hypothesis 2: A Cross-Culturally Uniform Developmental Sequence

Hypothesis 2 predicted that a cross-culturally uniform sequence of stages in the development of logical thinking would cause the same Guttman scales to function in Sweden and in India except for variation in rate from culture to culture.

Appendix V shows coefficients for ten Guttman scales. The coefficients for four groups—Swedish boys, Swedish girls, Swedish total and Indian boys—support hypothesis 2. The Hypothesis is supported not only when comparing Swedish boys to Indian boys, but also when comparing Swedish girls to Indian boys and when comparing the sexes in Sweden.

In one of the scales, GUTSC1B, the order of difficulty is reversed so that 1B:10 is the most difficult item in India and 1A:9 the most difficult one in Sweden. As both use the same cutting point (3) this neither supports nor rejects Hypothesis 2, but has to be regarded as a problem of "décalage" related to cultural differences between Sweden and India.

Hypothesis 3: Validity of the Theory-oriented Item Analysis

Hypothesis 3 predicted that different methods of test construction based on the Piagetian theory (an indirect approach through a series of Guttman scales, and a direct approach based on individual items) would be highly correlated with each other if the theory-oriented item analysis was valid.

Correlations between the Thinking test and the Reasoning Level test can be conceived of in two different ways:
1. as a test of the validity of the respective tests;
2. as a test of the validity of the theory-oriented item analysis which gave the three different weights that were assigned to the choice of distractors predicted to be chosen at different levels in the development of logical thinking: *1* for distractors hypothesized to correspond to pre-operational thinking; *2* for concrete operational thinking; and *3* for formal operational thinking.

Table 4.1. *Pearson Correlation Coefficients for Thinking x Reasoning Level*

Sample	N	Correlation coefficient
Sweden, boys	810	.90
Sweden, girls	733	.88
India, boys	719	.87

The data given in Table 4.1 support Hypothesis 3.

Hypothesis 4: Correlations with School Achievement

Hypothesis 4 predicted that the Guttman scales as well as the Thinking test and the Reasoning Level test would be positively correlated with measures of school achievement.

Twelve independent variables were used for testing Hypothesis 4: ten Guttman scales, the Thinking test and the Reasoning Level test. Eta correlation coefficients were calculated for correlations between an ordinal scale (the Guttman scales) as the independent variable and an interval scale as the dependent variable. Pearson correlation coefficients were computed for correlations between two interval scales.

Four measures were used as criteria of school achievement: Science I (IEA/1A, 1B), Science Minimized, the Word Knowledge test (IEA/2F), and the Reading Comprehension test (IEA/3C, 3D).

Appendix VI (Tables 4–6) shows Eta correlation coefficients for ten Guttman scales and four tests of school achievement.

Appendix VI (Tables 7–9) shows Pearson correlation coefficients for the Thinking test and the Reasoning Level test and the four tests of school achievement.

All correlation coefficients heavily support the hypothesis.

Hypothesis 5: Discriminating Power of the Guttman Scales

Hypothesis 5 predicted that (a) groups of individuals at different scale levels on the ten Guttman scales would be significantly different from each other, using tests of school achievement as criterion variables; and that (b) there would be a linear trend between the groups.

Hypothesis 5a was tested by using a one-way analysis of variance. The hypotheses tested were

H_0: there will be no significant difference between group means;

H_1: there will be a significant difference between group means.

Appendix VII (Tables 1–9) shows analyses of variance for ten Guttman scales and three tests of school achievement: Science I (IEA/1A, 1B), the Word Knowledge Test (IEA/2F), and the Reading Comprehension Test (IEA/3C, 3D).

H_1 was accepted for all scales and all criterion variables ($p > .01$).

Hypothesis 5b was tested by using the test of linearity (Ferguson, 1966, pp. 341–353). The hypotheses tested were

H_0: the variance of deviations from linearity is not significantly different from zero;

H_1: the variance of deviations from linearity is significantly different from zero.

Appendix VII (Tables 1–9) shows tests of linearity of the ten Guttman scales and the three tests of school achievement, as Hypothesis 5a. Appendix VII (Figures 1–10) shows relative frequencies at different levels of thinking (i.e., different scale types) in the Guttman scales and trends for three tests of school achievement as criterion variables.

H_0 was accepted for the tests of linearity, with only a few exceptions, showing slightly curvilinear trends.

Hypothesis 6: Type of Intelligence Measured

Hypothesis 6 was given two alternative forms, testing whether the ten Guttman scales, the Thinking test and the Reasoning Level test measured verbal intelligence or scientific intelligence.

Hypothesis 6a predicted that if the ten scales and two tests do measure some type of *verbal intelligence*, then the correlations would be higher with the two verbal intelligence tests than with the tests in science.

Hypothesis 6b, the alternative, predicted that if the ten scales and two tests do measure some type of *scientific intelligence* then correlations with a science test would be higher than with the verbal intelligence tests.

Twelve independent variables were used in testing Hypothesis 6: ten Guttman scales, the Thinking test and the Reasoning level test.

Four criterion variables were used as intelligence tests: (a) two tests of verbal intelligence–the Word Knowledge test (IEA/2F) and the Reading Comprehension Test (IEA/3C, 3D); and (b) two tests of scientific intelligence–Science I (IEA/1A, 1B) and Science Minimized.

Appendix VI (Tables 4–6) shows Eta correlation coefficients for ten Guttman scales and four intelligence tests. Appendix VI (Tables 7–9) shows Pearson correlation coefficients for the Thinking test, the Reasoning Level test and the four intelligence tests.

Tables 4.2–4.4 summarize the interpretations of the correlation coefficients in terms of percentage of the variance accounted for by different tests. (Ferguson, 1966, p. 126).

The data reject Hypothesis 6a and support Hypothesis 6b. The ten Guttman scales as well as the Thinking test and the Reasoning Level test do measure some type of scientific intelligence.

Table 4.2. *Percentage of Variance in Four Tests Explained by Ten Guttman Scales and Two Piaget Tests – Sweden, Boys*

	Verbal intelligence		Scientific intelligence	
	Word Knowledge	Reading Comprehension	Science I	Science Minimized
GUTSC1A	6	11	17	10
GUTSC1B	10	20	27	17
GUTSC2A	8	11	20	14
GUTSC2B	7	11	21	12
GUTSC2C	9	12	22	14
GUTSC2E	6	8	18	12
GUTSC3A	6	10	21	13
GUTSC3B	10	17	33	21
GUTSC3C	7	12	23	15
GUTSC3D	10	12	36	23
Thinking	15	26	47	29
Reasoning Level	15	28	48	29

Table 4.3. *Percentage of Variance in Four Tests Explained by Ten Guttman Scales and Two Piaget Tests – Sweden, Girls*

	Verbal intelligence		Scientific intelligence	
	Word Knowledge	Reading Comprehension	Science I	Science Minimized
GUTSC1A	6	9	21	12
GUTSC1B	9	13	27	15
GUTSC2A	3	3	12	5
GUTSC2B	5	5	16	7
GUTSC2C	2	4	15	6
GUTSC2E	2	3	14	7
GUTSC3A	4	11	18	11
GUTSC3B	6	15	26	16
GUTSC3C	5	11	19	11
GUTSC3D	7	15	27	16
Thinking	9	17	39	20
Reasoning Level	11	21	46	26

Table 4.4. *Percentage of Variance in Four Tests Explained by Ten Guttman Scales and Two Piaget Tests – India, Boys*

	Verbal intelligence		Scientific intelligence	
	Word Knowledge	Reading Comprehension	Science I	Science Minimized
GUTSC1A	10	4	22	13
GUTSC1B	13	9	34	21
GUTSC2A	15	8	25	16
GUTSC2B	18	12	32	21
GUTSC2C	12	9	25	15
GUTSC2E	7	3	17	10
GUTSC3A	10	7	13	7
GUTSC3B	7	4	18	10
GUTSC3C	10	8	16	9
GUTSC3D	7	4	23	13
Thinking	17	10	38	22
Reasoning Level	17	11	41	24

Chapter Five

Discussion

The present study was designed to investigate whether the logical model advanced by Jean Piaget could be regarded as a valid theoretical ground for didactic research in different subject matter areas. The results, which throughout strongly support the validity of the theory, seem to have important implications.

The construction of the two tests, the Thinking test and the Reasoning Level test, demonstrates not only that the logical model of Piaget can be used as a basis for test construction, but opens up as well the possibility of extending the series of surveys based on the IEA Six Subject Data Bank into an important new area awaiting investigation: that of the development of logical thinking among children in the 16 countries that participated in the Population I study.

The present study has demonstrated the occurrence of a fixed sequence in the development of logical thinking in Indian boys and Swedish boys and girls, thus proving the theory to be valid on this point. It should be noted that these findings are obtained from countries which differ greatly in language and culture, which encourages further cross-national surveys of the type suggested above.

The present study has also demonstrated the didactic importance of the new variable called "scientific intelligence." The international survey suggested above could focus on individual differences in this variable. It could study how the development of logical thinking is related to individual variables pertaining to home background and to perception of the mother tongue. The survey could also investigate how scientific intelligence is related to methods of instruction and types of curricula.

In such a study it would be important to take the necessary steps ensuing from the finding of the present study—namely,that groups of illiterates had been included in the sample. This illustrates the necessity of controlling the implicit assumption that all the students understand the test questions.

A study of logical thinking in 16 countries using IEA data would be truly interdisciplinary, because the same students were tested on Science, Reading Comprehension and Word Knowledge. A study of achievements at different levels of thinking, comparing different types of performance, would be of prime importance. Another basic problem would be a study of the relationship between attitudes and development of logical thinking, an area to which very little attention has been paid in the field of Piagetian studies, owing to the lack of cognitive and affective data from the same individuals. The lack of studies in this problem area has been acutely felt. (See, for instance, Hunt, 1961; Flavell, 1963, p. 421.)

Piaget (1966), in expressing his view of the need and meaning of comparative studies in genetic psychology, interpreted the constant and necessary order of stages of development of "operative intelligence" as being explained by "biological factors depending on the 'epigenetic' system (maturation of the nervous system, etc.)". He predicts that comparative studies will make it possible to study four groups of factors that influence the development of logical thinking: (1) biological factors; (2) factors corresponding to individual interaction with the physical environment; (3) factors corresponding to inter-individual interaction, i.e., general socialization factors; and (4) educational factors.

An international survey of logical thinking mentioned above could come very close to the aims described by Piaget.

General Structures and the Testing of Religious Thinking

The main problem encountered in the attempts to apply the Piagetian theory within the classroom has been the *lack of test instruments* to obtain reliable measures of individual differences in the development of logical thinking. Some recent articles show how seriously this lack of instruments is felt. Fogelman (1969) as well as Weisman and Safford (1971) discuss the use of single Piagetian tasks within the classroom—in order to get rough classifications on stages of thinking—and they regret the difficulties, especially the low reliability, of such measures.

The procedures of test construction tried out in the present study show new methods for designing Piagetian tests by means of multiple-choice items. Since it takes Piaget's logical model and not single Piagetian tasks as a starting point, it has the advantage of having a scientific language which can be applied in all subject areas in the design of test items. The Thinking and the Reasoning Level tests will also provide the criterion measures to be used at validation of future Piagetian tests, until a complete Piaget-test can be designed using the principles and methods of the present study. As the items of these two tests already are available within the Science test (IEA/1A, 1B) in 16 countries, research workers can start using them as reference points in educational research.

A fundamental concept of Piaget's theory is that of "general structure." The construction of the logical model was an attempt at describing such a general structure in the development of logical thinking. The distinction between the structure of thinking and the object of thinking makes testing of such a general structure important in all curricular areas. Let us here illustrate the problem with one subject area, that of instruction in religion.

Within the theoretical framework of Piagetian theory R. Goldman has been the most influential scholar of student predispositions towards instruction in religion. His basic view is "that religious thinking is no different in mode and method from non-religious thinking." Using the traditional interview method on religious stories, he found support for Piaget's three stages in the realm of religious thinking (Goldman, 1964, pp. 4, 51–67). His findings have been confirmed by Martinsson (1968) and Pettersson (1970).

Goldman agrees with Piaget that the same "general structure" is at work in religious thinking as in non-religious thinking. Consequently test construction within the field of religious thinking could be based on the same theoretical ground as in all other subject areas.

The construction of a test battery, composed of subtests from the fields of Religious Knowledge, Science, Mathematics, and Literature, would enable us to study a number of important problems of Piagetian theory as related to Religious thinking. First, it would be possible to investigate the validity of the theory that the same "general structure" is at work in all subject areas. Secondly, the "profiles" of thinking in different subject areas could be studied, and the old problem of time lag ("décalage") between logically similar problems could be extended to comparisons between subject areas. Finally, these two problems are closely related to the basic theoretical question: is the development of thinking parallel and consequent from one subject-matter field to another? If so this would prove the development of thinking to be such a "general structure" and would mean that, consequently, measurements of development of thinking in one subject area could be used for development of instruction in another.

The two preceeding parts of the discussion of the findings have focused on two major topics:

1. a proposed international survey of the development of logical thinking;
2. ideas for future test construction in different subject matter fields, with special reference to religious thinking.

The very last part of this discussion will focus on

3. implications of the test construction for future research in education.

Testing the Process of Thinking —Not Simply the Products of Thinking

Cronbach (1970, p. 32) has stressed the distinction between process and product, pointing out that most psychometric testing concerns itself with the product of performance and only rarely with the process. An international conference on practical testing, basic studies of cognitive development from psychological and anthropological perspectives, held in Istanbul, Turkey, 1971, emphasized "that a better research foundation for inference about processes is needed" (Cronbach and Drenth, 1972, p. 471), and Eckensberger (1972) stressed the need of a theory for applied cross-cultural study of the process of thinking. Eckensberger mentioned three basic requirements of a theory useful for this type of investigation: (1) it should be formulated independent of a special sample, (2) it should contain explicit assumptions about interaction between the individual and his environment, and (3) it should be developmental in nature. A theory that filled these requirements was that of Piaget.

The present study has shown that it is possible to make inferences from performance in multiple-choice items to the process of thinking as described by Piaget—which has made it feasible to validate Piagetian findings based on clinical interviews, summarized in his logical model, against performance on objective tests as external criteria. Thus, the new variables, the Thinking test and the Reasoning Level test, can be regarded as process measures of thinking.

These measures of the development of logical thinking can be used for research purposes in three problem areas:

1. As dependent variables in studies of the effects of environmental factors and methods of instruction on the level of thinking;
2. As independent variables in studies of scholastic performance;
3. In multivariate model building focusing on didactic processes.

Appendices

Test Items – Swedish Version

IEA/1A:8

Jan ville undersöka vilken av tre jordtyper - lera, sand eller matjord - som var bäst för att odla bönor i. Han fyllde tre blomkrukor med olika jordtyper och planterade sedan samma antal bönor i varje, så som bilden visar. Han ställde krukorna sida vid sida på fönsterbrädet och vattnade alla tre lika mycket.

Varför var Jans experiment INTE lämpligt i det här fallet?

A. Växterna i en av krukorna fick mer solljus än växterna i de övriga.
B. Mängden jord var inte densamma i krukorna.
C. En av krukorna skulle ha placerats i mörker.
D. Jan skulle ha använt tre sorters frön.
E. Det skulle bli för varmt på fönsterbrädet.

IEA/1A:9

Johan lade några frön på en fuktig bomullstuss i en skål. Bredvid Johans skål lade Eva några likadana frön i ett glas fyllt med vatten. Efter två dagar grodde Johans frön men inget hände med Evas. Vilken av följande förklaringar är mest trolig?

A. Evas frön hade fått torka för länge.
B. Eva lät inte sina frön få tillräckligt med luft.
C. Eva ställde inte sitt glas på ett tillräckligt varmt ställe.
D. Eva skulle ha använt ett annat slags frö.
E. Eva använde inte en bomullstuss.

IEA/1A:10

Görans katt skadades av en bil och blev halt. Några månader efter olyckan födde hon en kull ungar. Vilken av meningarna beskriver hur ungarna troligen såg ut?

A. Alla var halta därför att modern var det.
B. De flesta var halta, men inte alla eftersom fadern inte var halt.
C. De flesta var inte halta därför att fadern inte var halt.
D. Ingen var halt eftersom moderns skada berodde på en olycka.
E. Bara en var halt därför att modern var halt.

IEA/1A:14

Karin och Agneta köpte båda samma slags gummiboll. Karin sa: "Min boll studsar högre än din". Agneta svarade: "Bevisa det om du kan." Vad skulle Karin göra?

A. Släppa båda bollarna från samma höjd och se vilken som studsar högst.
B. Kasta båda bollarna mot en vägg och se hur långt varje boll studsar från väggen.
C. Släppa båda bollarna från olika höjd och se vilken, som studsar högst.
D. Kasta bollarna mot golvet och se hur högt de studsar.
E. Känna på bollarna med handen för att ta reda på vilken som är hårdast.

IEA/1A:16

Britt ville gunga med sin lillebror Göran. Vilken bild visar det bästa sättet för Britt, som vägde 40 kg, att balansera Göran, som vägde 20 kg?

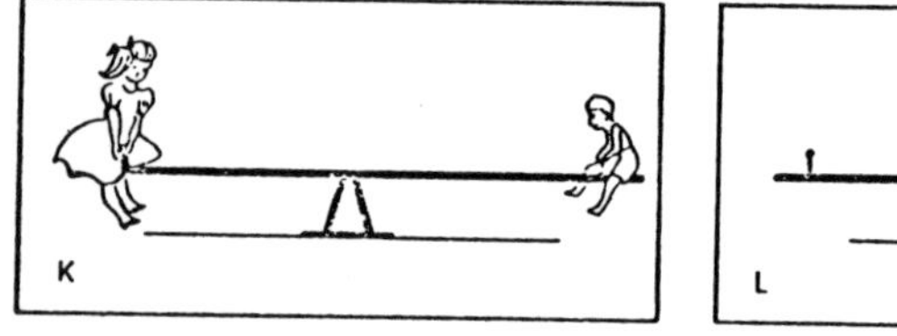

A. Bild K.
B. Bild L.
C. Bild M.
D. Bild N.
E. Ingen av bilderna.

IEA/1A:20

Lennart undrade om ljud kan gå genom vatten. För att få reda på det skulle han kunna göra ett av följande experiment. Vilket?

A. Slå ihop två stenar i en vattenstråle.
B. Slå ihop två stenar ovanför vattenytan i en sjö eller simbassäng och lyssna på ljudet.
C. Hålla örat nära vattenytan i en sjö eller simbassäng och slå ihop två stenar ovan vattnet.
D. Hålla huvudet under vattnet i en sjö eller simbassäng och slå ihop två stenar i vattnet.
E. Släppa en sten i vattnet och lyssna efter plasket.

IEA/1B:10

Några frön gror bäst i mörker, andra bäst där det är ljust medan en del gror lika bra i mörker som i ljus. Om du ville ta reda på till vilket slag en speciell sorts frö hör skulle du kunna så en del av fröna på ett fuktigt läskpapper och

A. lägga dem på ett varmt och mörkt ställe.
B. lägga en bit av papperet på ett ljust ställe och en annan bit på ett mörkt ställe.
C. lägga dem på ett varmt och ljust ställe.
D. så resten av fröna på ett torrt läskpapper och lägga dem på ett ljust ställe.
E. så resten av fröna på ett torrt läskpapper och lägga dem på ett mörkt ställe.

Appendix I.2

Test Items – Hindi Version

IEA/1A:8

8. राम यह अध्ययन करना चाहता था कि चिकनी, रेतीली या दोमट इन तीन प्रकार की मिट्टी में से कौन सी सेम उगाने के लिए सबसे अच्छी होगी। जैसा कि चित्र में दिखाया गया है, उसने तीन गमले लिए और प्रत्येक में भिन्न-भिन्न प्रकार की मिट्टी भरी और प्रत्येक गमले में बराबर संख्या में सेम के बीज बोये। उसने उनको खिड़की के पाट पर अगल-बगल रख दिया और प्रत्येक गमले में समान मात्रा में पानी डाला।

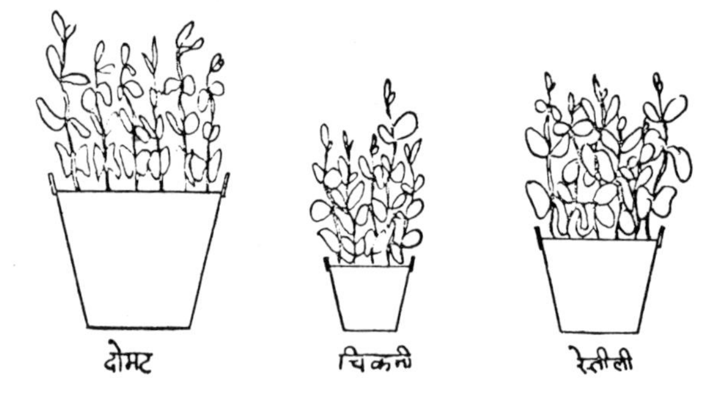

तुम्हारे विचार में राम का प्रयोग उसके ध्येय के विचार से क्यों अच्छा नहीं था ?

क एक गमले के पौधों को दूसरे गमले के पौधों की अपेक्षा अधिक प्रकाश मिला।
ख प्रत्येक गमले में मिटटी की मात्रा समान नहीं थी।
ग एक गमले को अंधेरे में रखना चाहिए था।
घ राम को विभिन्न मात्रा में जल का प्रयोग करना चाहिये था।
च पौधों को खिड़की के पाट पर अधिक गर्मी मिली होगी।

IEA/1A:9

9. गोपाल ने कुछ बीज तश्तरी में गीली रुई के ऊपर रखे। रमा ने उसी प्रकार के कुछ बीज पानी भरे गिलास में उस के एक ओर रख दिये। दो दिन पश्चात् गोपाल के बीज अंकुरित हो गये परन्तु रमा के बीजों को कुछ नहीं हुआ। निम्नलिखित में से कौन सी इसकी संभावित व्याख्या है ?

   क रमा के बीज बहुत अधिक समय तक सूखे रखे गये थे।
   ख रमा ने अपने बीजों को पर्याप्त वायु नहीं मिलने दी।
   ग रमा ने गिलास को पर्याप्त गर्म स्थान पर नहीं रखा।
   घ रमा को अन्य प्रकार के बीजों का प्रयोग करना चाहिये था।
   च रमा ने कैसी भी रुई का प्रयोग नहीं किया।

IEA/1A:10

10. गोपाल की पालतू मादा खरगोश को कार से चोट पहुँची और वह लंगड़ी हो गई। दुर्घटना के कुछ महीने पश्चात् उसने बच्चे दिये। निम्नलिखित में से कौन सा कथन उसकी व्याख्या करता है कि बच्चे किस प्रकार के होंगे ?

   क सब लंगड़े होंगे क्योंकि उनकी मां भी लंगड़ी थी।
   ख उनमें से अधिकांश लंगड़े होंगे परन्तु सब नहीं, क्योंकि उसका पिता लंगडा नहीं था।
   ग उनमें से अधिकांश लंगड़े नहीं होंगे क्योंकि पिता लंगड़ा नहीं था।
   घ उनमें से कोई लंगड़ा नहीं होगा क्योंकि माँ का लंगड़ापन एक दुर्घटना के कारण था।
   च केवल एक लंगड़ा होगा क्योंकि माँ लंगड़ी थी।

IEA/1A:14

14. ऊषा और रमा प्रत्येक ने एक ही प्रकार की रबड़ की गेंद खरीदी। ऊषा ने कहा, "मेरी गेंद तुम्हारी गेंद की अपेक्षा अच्छी उछलती है।" रमा ने उत्तर दिया, "मैं चाहती हूँ कि तुम इसको सिद्ध करके दिखाओ।" ऊषा को क्या करना चाहिए ?

   क दोनों गेंदों को एक ही ऊँचाई से छोड़कर देखें कि कौन सी गेंद अधिक ऊँची उछलती है।
   ख दोनों गेंदों को दीवार में मार कर देखें कि प्रत्येक गेंद दीवार से कितनी दूर उछलती है।
   ग दोनों गेंदों को विभिन्न ऊँचाई से छोड़कर देखें कि कौन सी गेंद अधिक ऊँची उछलती है।
   घ गेंदों को नीचे फर्श पर मारकर देखें कि वे कितनी ऊँची उछलती हैं।
   च गेंदों को हाथ से स्पर्श कर यह पता लगाना चाहिए कि कौन सी गेंद अधिक कठोर है।

IEA/1A:16

16. रमा अपने छोटे भाई कृष्ण के साथ तखते पर झूलना चाहती थी। रमा के 100 पौंड भार और कृष्ण के 50 पौंड भार को संतुलित करने के लिए निम्नलिखित में से कौनसा चित्र सबसे ठीक स्थिति दिखाता है ?

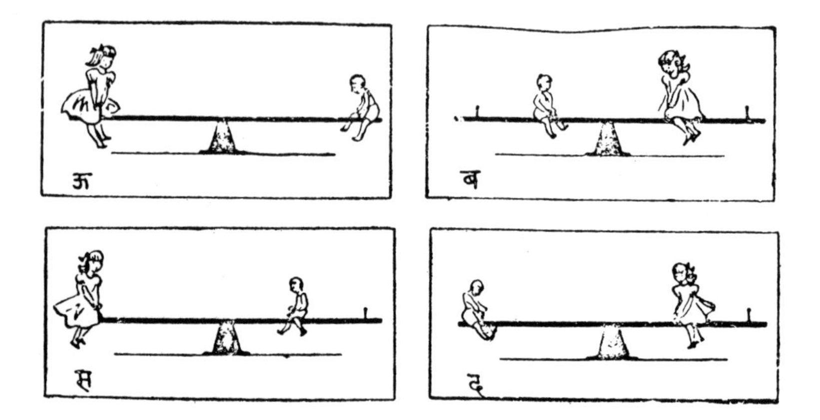

क चित्र अ।
ख चित्र ब।
ग चित्र स।
घ चित्र द।
च इनमें से कोई नहीं।

IEA/1A:20

20. विजय यह जानने के लिये इच्छुक था कि क्या ध्वनि जल में चल सकती है। प्रयोग द्वारा यह जानने के लिए निम्नलिखित में से उसे क्या करना चाहिए ?

क दो पत्थरों को जल की धारा में टकराये।
ख झील या तालाब के जल के ऊपर दो पत्थरों को टकराये और उत्पन्न ध्वनि को सुने।
ग अपना कान झील या तालाब के जल के ऊपर लगाये और दो पत्थरों को जल के अन्दर टकराये।
घ अपना सिर झील या तालाब के जल के नीचे रखे और दो पत्थरों को जल के अन्दर टकराये।
च जल में पत्थर फेंक कर लहरों की आवाज़ को सुने।

10. कुछ बीज अंधेरे में अंकुरित होते हैं और कुछ प्रकाश में, जब कि कुछ बीज अंधेरे या प्रकाश दोनों में ही समान रूप से अंकुरित होते हैं। यदि तुम प्रयोग द्वारा यह जानना चाहो कि एक विशेष प्रकार का बीज कौन से वर्ग से सम्बन्धित है तो तुम कुछ बीजों को भीगे सोख्ते कागज पर बोओगे और

    क अंधेरे में गर्म स्थान पर रखोगे।
    ख एक समूह को अंधेरे में और दूसरे समूह को प्रकाश में रखोगे।
    ग प्रकाश में गर्म स्थान पर रखोगे।
    घ कुछ बीज सूखे सोख्ते कागज पर बोकर प्रकाश में रखोगे।
    च कुछ बीजों को सूखे कागज पर बोकर अंधेरे में रखोगे।

Test Items – English Version

IEA/1A:8

Tom wanted to learn which of three types of soil - clay, sand or loam - would be best for growing beans. He found three flower-pots, put a different type of soil in each pot, and planted the same number of beans in each, as shown in the drawing. He placed them side by side on the window sill and gave each pot the same amount of water.

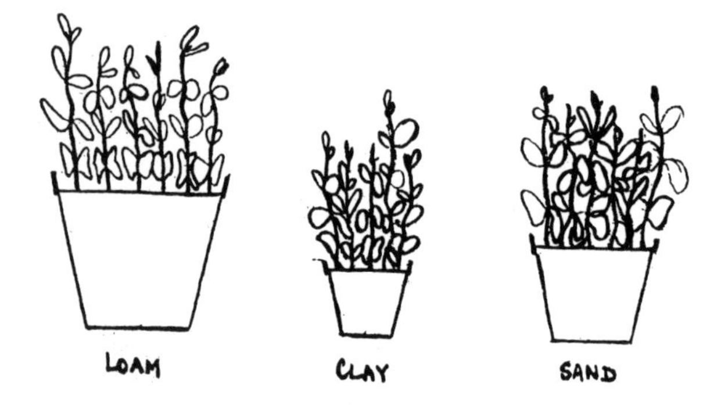

Why was Tom's experiment NOT a good one for his purpose?

A. The plants in one pot got more sunlight than the plants in the other pots.
B. The amount of soil in each pot was not the same.
C. One pot should have been placed in the dark.
D. Tom should have used different amounts of water.
E. It would get too hot on the window sill.

IEA/1A:9

John put some seeds on moist cotton wool in a dish. Jane put some seeds of the same kind into a glass full of water by the side of his. After two days John's seeds sprouted but nothing seemed to happen to Jane's. Which of the following is the most probable explanation?

A. Jane's seeds had been kept dry for too long.
B. Jane did not allow her seeds enough air.
C. Jane did not put the glass in a warm enough place.
D. Jane should have used a different kind of seed.
E. Jane did not use any cotton wool.

IEA/1A:10

John's pet rabbit was injured by a car and became lame. Some months after the accident she produced a litter. Which of the following describes what the babies would probably be like?

A. All of them would be lame because the mother was.
B. Most of them would be lame but not all of them because the father was not lame.
C. Most of them would not be lame because the father was not lame.
D. None of them would be lame because the mother's lameness was due to an accident.
E. Only one of them would be lame because the mother was lame.

IEA/1A:14

Mary and Jane each bought the same kind of rubber ball. Mary said, "My ball bounces better than yours." Jane replied, "I'd like to see you prove that." What should Mary do?

A. Drop both balls from the same hight and notice which bounces higher.
B. Throw both balls against a wall and see how far each ball bounces off the wall.
C. Drop the two balls from different heights and notice which bounces higher.
D. Throw the balls down against the floor and see how high they bounce.
E. Feel the balls by hand to find which is the harder.

IEA/1A:16

Betty wanted to seesaw with her little brother, George. Which picture shows the best way for Betty, who weighed 100 pounds, to balance George, who weighed 50 pounds?

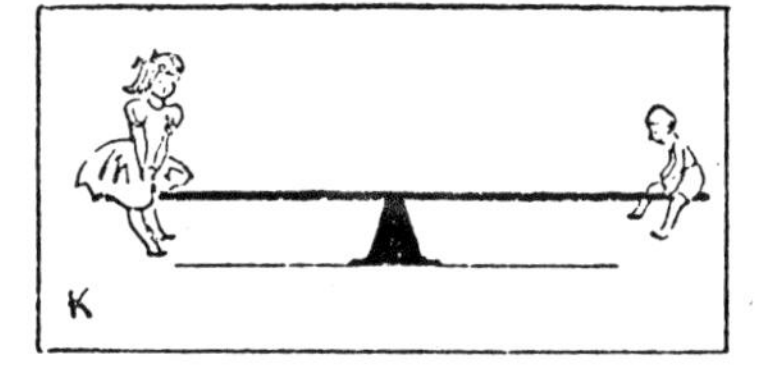

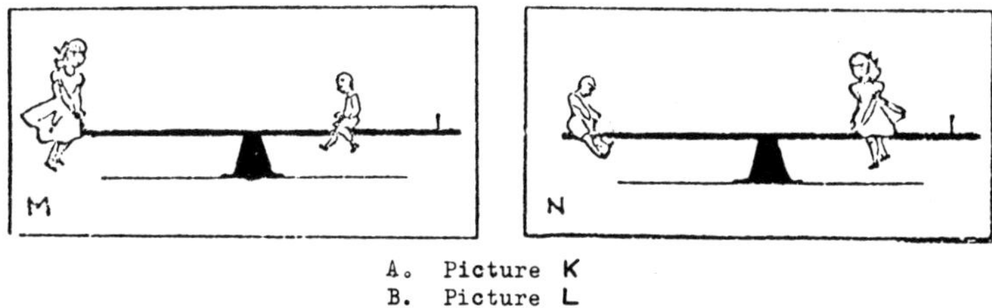

A. Picture K
B. Picture L
C. Picture M
D. Picture N
E. None of these

IEA/1A:20

Harry wondered if sound is able to travel through water. To find out by an experiment which of the following should he do?

A. Hit two stones together in a jet of water.
B. Hit two stones together above the water of a lake or swimming pool and listen to the sound.
C. Put his ear next to the water of a lake or swimming pool and hit two stones together above the water.
D. Put his head under the water of a lake or swimming pool and hit two stones together in the water.
E. Drop a stone into the water and listen for the splash.

IEA/1B:10

Some seeds germinate best in the dark, others in the light, while others germinate equally well in the dark or the light. If you wanted to find out by means of an experiment to which group a certain kind of seed belonged, you would sow some of the seeds on damp blotting paper and

A. keep them in a warm place in the dark.
B. keep one batch in the light and another in the dark.
C. keep them in a warm place in the light.
D. sow some on dry blotting paper and keep them in the light.
E. sow some on dry blotting paper and keep them in the dark.

Anova Tables – Item IEA/1A:16

Three Groups Classified on the Basis of
Choice of Distractor in the Item
(Sample and Dependent Variable are given in Table Headings)

Table II.1 *India, Boys – Reading Comprehension Corrected Score*

Source of variation	Sum of squares	Degrees of freedom	Variance estimate
Between	3373.19	2	1686.59
Within	47894.50	733	65.34
Total	51267.69	735	F = 25.81 ***

Table II.2 *India, Boys – Word Knowledge Corrected Score*

Source of variation	Sum of squares	Degrees of freedom	Variance estimate
Between	7209.50	2	3604.75
Within	75596.25	733	103.13
Total	82805.75	735	F = 34.95 ***

Table II.3 *India, Boys – Science Total Corrected Score*

Source of variation	Sum of squares	Degrees of freedom	Variance estimate
Between	6288.19	2	3144.09
Within	32546.25	733	44.40
Total	38834.44	735	F = 70.81 ***

Table II.4 *Sweden, Boys - Reading Comprehension Corrected Score*

Source of variation	Sum of squares	Degrees of freedom	Variance estimate
Between	4438.50	2	2219.25
Within	82639.56	820	100.78
Total	87078.06	822	F = 22.02 ***

Table II.5 *Sweden, Boys - Word Knowledge Corrected Score*

Source of variation	Sum of squares	Degrees of freedom	Variance estimate
Between	2052.19	2	1026.10
Within	47015.38	820	57.34
Total	49067.56	822	F = 17.90 ***

Table II.6 *Sweden, Boys - Science Total Corrected Score*

Source of variation	Sum of squares	Degrees of freedom	Variance estimate
Between	4950.63	2	2475.32
Within	35555.50	820	43.36
Total	40506.13	822	F = 57.08 ***

Table II.7 *Sweden, Girls - Reading Comprehension Corrected Score*

Source of variation	Sum of squares	Degrees of freedom	Variance estimate
Between	1793.50	2	896.75
Within	58642.00	744	78.82
Total	60435.50	746	F = 11.38 ***

Table II.8 *Sweden, Girls - Word Knowledge Corrected Score*

Source of variation	Sum of squares	Degrees of freedom	Variance estimate
Between	664.63	2	332.31
Within	37356.13	744	50.21
Total	38020.75	746	F = 6.62 **

Table II.9 *Sweden, Girls - Science Total Corrected Score*

Source of variation	Sum of squares	Degrees of freedom	Variance estimate
Between	3478.25	2	1739.13
Within	28070.94	744	37.73
Total	31549.19	746	F = 46.09 ***

Appendix III

Criterion-Related Item Analysis Data

Table III.1 *Criterion-related Item Analysis Data, India, Boys, IEA/lA:8*

Grade 3

Answers		A	B	C	D	E
	n	26	49	32	41	21
	%	15	29	19	24	12
WKC	$\bar{X}$	11.12	12.78	11.45	16.32	12.53
	s	8.54	10.53	9.56	11.93	8.09
RCC	$\bar{X}$	7.78	11.24	12.22	14.02	9.09
	s	5.66	6.69	8.03	10.52	6.37

No answer: 4

Grade 4

Answers		A	B	C	D	E
	n	52	81	30	88	41
	%	18	28	10	30	14
WKC	$\bar{X}$	13.49	14.78	12.77	16.59	8.70
	s	10.29	11.81	8.48	11.07	8.34
RCC	$\bar{X}$	11.57	13.25	11.05	14.64	7.66
	s	6.63	7.52	7.33	10.01	6.00

No answer: 9

Grade 5

Answers		A	B	C	D	E
	n	63	90	34	88	39
	%	20	29	11	28	12
WKC	$\bar{X}$	14.40	15.82	12.80	20.80	12.47
	s	10.20	9.87	10.67	10.91	9.89
RCC	$\bar{X}$	11.63	15.10	11.94	17.03	9.38
	s	5.38	7.62	8.34	10.47	6.80

No answer: 11

Grade 6

Answers		A	B	C	D	E
	n	19	32	2	26	16
	%	20	34	2	27	17
WKC	$\bar{X}$	18.12	18.34	12.00	17.77	11.07
	s	13.72	7.48	2.83	8.31	8.18
RCC	$\bar{X}$	8.74	12.07	12.35	13.69	7.39
	s	6.96	7.51	4.74	7.95	4.44

No answer: 3

Table III.2 *Criterion-related Item Analysis Data, India, Boys, IEA/1A:9*

Grade 3

Answers		A	B	C	D	E
	n	22	59	21	22	45
	%	13	35	12	13	27
WKC	$\bar{X}$	10.78	14.33	8.21	8.51	17.03
	s	8.39	9.21	9.39	8.68	11.71
RCC	$\bar{X}$	9.36	13.30	7.50	7.30	12.90
	s	6.17	7.79	5.74	6.93	9.27

No answer: 4

Grade 4

Answers		A	B	C	D	E
	n	44	118	27	44	66
	%	15	39	9	15	22
WKC	$\bar{X}$	12.41	18.49	8.98	7.97	13.60
	s	8.79	10.76	9.18	8.97	10.70
RCC	$\bar{X}$	12.11	15.99	7.62	8.69	10.79
	s	7.05	8.73	6.64	6.09	7.88

No answer: 2

Grade 5

Answers		A	B	C	D	E
	n	70	121	34	25	72
	%	22	38	11	8	22
WKC	$\bar{X}$	15.65	19.85	13.68	11.57	14.15
	s	9.27	11.03	9.11	10.39	10.11
RCC	$\bar{X}$	10.31	17.51	10.48	10.96	13.85
	s	5.41	9.26	7.32	6.33	8.13

No answer: 3

Grade 6

Answers		A	B	C	D	E
	n	13	45	9	14	13
	%	14	48	10	15	14
WKC	$\bar{X}$	11.85	21.42	14.56	11.94	12.69
	s	7.26	9.32	5.34	10.47	7.08
RCC	$\bar{X}$	10.48	12.80	10.71	9.38	8.54
	s	6.76	8.42	6.62	6.53	4.94

No answer: 4

Table III.3 *Criterion-related Item Analysis Data, India, Boys, IEA/1A:10*

Grade 3

Answers		A	B	C	D	E
	n	15	18	14	103	18
	%	9	11	8	61	11
WKC	$\bar{X}$	9.80	12.17	8.66	16.24	5.18
	s	6.19	8.15	8.16	10.38	5.39
RCC	$\bar{X}$	5.38	9.46	9.91	13.67	6.15
	s	4.28	7.20	5.47	8.51	4.29

No answer: 5

Grade 4

Answers		A	B	C	D	E
	n	20	22	35	184	33
	%	7	7	12	63	11
WKC	$\bar{X}$	9.61	8.29	8.30	18.04	6.35
	s	7.20	10.34	7.41	10.45	7.33
RCC	$\bar{X}$	6.98	8.16	7.36	15.49	7.91
	s	5.96	7.24	6.62	7.97	6.43

No answer: 7

Grade 5

Answers		A	B	C	D	E
	n	11	33	35	218	26
	%	3	10	11	67	8
WKC	$\bar{X}$	7.19	14.49	13.06	18.19	10.12
	s	8.59	9.13	9.21	10.95	6.69
RCC	$\bar{X}$	3.92	11.08	10.55	15.64	9.67
	s	3.29	6.58	6.70	8.49	7.59

No answer: 2

Grade 6

Answers		A	B	C	D	E
	n	6	2	8	76	4
	%	6	2	8	79	4
WKC	$\bar{X}$	15.83	13.50	13.39	17.83	10.00
	s	6.79	2.12	8.47	9.85	6.06
RCC	$\bar{X}$	7.95	9.65	7.54	11.76	9.82
	s	8.29	.92	5.70	7.71	3.46

No answer: 2

Table III.4 *Criterion-related Item Analysis Data, India, Boys, IEA/1A:14*

Grade 3

Answers		A	B	C	D	E
	n	59	20	21	24	45
	%	35	12	12	14	27
WKC	$\bar{X}$	13.97	9.11	7.87	12.30	16.36
	s	9.49	9.53	7.16	10.24	11.60
RCC	$\bar{X}$	12.79	7.64	8.31	9.24	13.24
	s	6.80	6.90	6.22	8.00	9.91

No answer: 4

Grade 4

Answers		A	B	C	D	E
	n	110	31	32	43	83
	%	37	10	11	14	28
WKC	$\bar{X}$	18.51	10.30	9.89	12.40	12.10
	s	10.79	7.69	11.90	10.46	9.72
RCC	$\bar{X}$	14.56	7.99	8.22	11.74	13.12
	s	8.56	5.94	6.56	7.63	8.81

No answer: 2

Grade 5

Answers		A	B	C	D	E
	n	116	26	32	36	108
	%	36	8	10	11	34
WKC	$\bar{X}$	18.96	12.47	11.85	14.36	16.41
	s	11.31	9.62	10.52	9.66	9.99
RCC	$\bar{X}$	15.70	8.40	11.29	11.31	14.89
	s	8.50	5.29	6.58	8.36	8.86

No answer: 7

Grade 6

Answers		A	B	C	D	E
	n	32	6	8	13	38
	%	33	6	8	13	39
WKC	$\bar{X}$	19.69	12.02	16.00	12.93	16.66
	s	9.54	11.98	5.78	7.88	9.69
RCC	$\bar{X}$	11.28	12.38	10.42	8.85	11.57
	s	8.18	8.12	7.07	5.00	7.56

No answer: 1

Table III.5 *Criterion-related Item Analysis Data, India, Boys, IEA/1A:16*

Grade 3

Answers		A	B	C	D	E
	n	16	16	28	77	25
	%	10	10	17	48	15
WKC	$\bar{X}$	11.06	8.51	11.51	16.51	7.54
	s	8.47	6.80	10.63	10.76	8.58
RCC	$\bar{X}$	8.56	8.30	10.01	13.75	7.58
	s	4.17	5.94	8.13	8.94	6.20

No answer: 11

Grade 4

Answers		A	B	C	D	E
	n	37	26	45	133	43
	%	13	9	16	47	15
WKC	$\bar{X}$	10.03	9.63	18.58	16.85	8.85
	s	8.60	9.67	11.86	10.47	9.13
RCC	$\bar{X}$	10.50	10.17	13.13	14.49	7.09
	s	5.91	7.07	7.27	9.27	6.71

No answer: 17

Grade 5

Answers		A	B	C	D	E
	n	45	39	54	132	33
	%	15	13	18	44	11
WKC	$\bar{X}$	10.98	12.07	18.04	19.01	17.18
	s	8.39	11.41	10.81	10.20	10.69
RCC	$\bar{X}$	11.26	11.35	12.83	16.65	13.00
	s	6.21	7.34	7.70	9.06	9.15

No answer: 22

Grade 6

Answers		A	B	C	D	E
	n	15	12	10	49	9
	%	16	13	11	52	9
WKC	$\bar{X}$	12.47	11.75	10.41	21.49	13.12
	s	8.08	4.58	8.51	8.94	9.58
RCC	$\bar{X}$	8.45	7.26	8.30	13.97	8.01
	s	6.19	3.72	6.05	8.03	5.34

No answer: 3

Table III.6 *Criterion-related Item Analysis Data, India, Boys, IEA/1A:20*

Grade 3

Answers		A	B	C	D	E
	n	10	24	41	32	54
	%	6	15	25	20	34
WKC	$\bar{X}$	6.72	12.88	17.03	13.23	11.54
	s	12.27	8.97	13.35	9.40	7.74
RCC	$\bar{X}$	7.76	8.95	14.47	10.96	10.84
	s	6.04	6.01	10.27	8.09	6.96

No answer: 12

Grade 4

Answers		A	B	C	D	E
	n	27	27	65	75	92
	%	9	9	23	26	32
WKC	$\bar{X}$	14.12	15.89	15.90	16.42	10.77
	s	9.54	10.13	11.07	11.79	10.15
RCC	$\bar{X}$	10.11	9.21	15.81	12.24	12.28
	s	7.30	7.19	9.23	8.76	7.62

No answer: 15

Grade 5

Answers		A	B	C	D	E
	n	19	34	59	80	113
	%	6	11	19	26	37
WKC	$\bar{X}$	16.22	17.12	17.65	19.89	12.85
	s	8.90	9.18	11.89	10.82	10.10
RCC	$\bar{X}$	14.33	11.62	15.16	17.08	11.78
	s	5.73	6.57	10.70	9.45	6.84

No answer: 20

Grade 6

Answers		A	B	C	D	E
	n	8	9	11	28	37
	%	9	10	12	30	40
WKC	$\bar{X}$	13.25	13.22	16.27	21.29	16.14
	s	5.42	9.77	7.51	11.50	8.12
RCC	$\bar{X}$	8.16	10.32	12.60	10.58	12.13
	s	8.87	7.52	8.31	6.70	7.67

No answer: 5

Table III.7 *Criterion-related Item Analysis Data, India, Boys, IEA/1B:10*

Grade 3

Answers		A	B	C	D	E
	n	16	50	50	31	21
	%	10	30	30	18	13
WKC	$\bar{X}$	11.69	15.80	10.25	16.53	8.91
	s	5.42	9.98	8.84	13.56	8.15
RCC	$\bar{X}$	6.04	11.96	12.09	14.07	6.33
	s	5.10	6.87	7.95	10.36	5.59

No answer: 5

Grade 4

Answers		A	B	C	D	E
	n	47	91	80	42	31
	%	16	31	27	14	11
WKC	$\bar{X}$	11.92	16.34	12.35	14.39	15.43
	s	9.68	10.82	11.27	11.52	10.42
RCC	$\bar{X}$	10.07	13.83	13.05	11.63	12.07
	s	6.90	8.12	9.10	9.11	8.05

No answer: 10

Grade 5

Answers		A	B	C	D	E
	n	33	108	92	45	40
	%	10	34	29	14	13
WKC	$\bar{X}$	11.52	17.67	19.78	14.05	10.36
	s	10.72	10.08	10.31	10.56	9.18
RCC	$\bar{X}$	12.10	12.90	16.45	15.44	9.13
	s	7.27	7.42	10.11	8.78	5.09

No answer: 7

Grade 6

Answers		A	B	C	D	E
	n	10	38	26	9	12
	%	11	40	27	9	13
WKC	$\bar{X}$	15.30	21.34	13.86	12.11	12.26
	s	6.09	9.53	9.87	5.33	8.91
RCC	$\bar{X}$	6.65	14.30	9.28	9.76	8.91
	s	5.76	7.84	6.70	6.89	5.38

No answer: 3

Table III.8 *Criterion-related Item Analysis Data, Sweden, Boys and Girls, IEA/1A:8*

Boys, Grade 3

Answers		A	B	C	D	E
	n	60	174	50	56	70
	%	15	42	12	14	17
WKC	$\bar{X}$	13.85	14.60	10.01	13.29	14.06
	s	6.60	8.03	6.97	7.62	7.38
RCC	$\bar{X}$	17.54	22.83	15.91	17.27	19.13
	s	9.37	10.74	9.14	9.15	9.77

No answer: 12

Boys, Grade 4

Answers		A	B	C	D	E
	n	72	261	46	32	50
	%	16	57	10	7	11
WKC	$\bar{X}$	15.14	17.04	14.76	13.97	12.61
	s	7.13	7.47	7.10	6.86	8.61
RCC	$\bar{X}$	20.85	26.53	20.33	18.46	19.97
	s	10.87	9.17	9.44	8.76	10.66

No answer: 6

Girls, Grade 3

Answers		A	B	C	D	E
	n	64	186	44	44	49
	%	17	48	11	11	13
WKC	$\bar{X}$	13.13	13.92	11.60	10.46	11.68
	s	7.29	7.02	7.56	6.21	7.15
RCC	$\bar{X}$	20.61	23.28	17.07	14.82	18.10
	s	9.33	9.18	10.09	9.27	8.82

No answer: 21

Girls, Grade 4

Answers		A	B	C	D	E
	n	69	236	50	39	60
	%	15	52	11	9	13
WKC	$\bar{X}$	13.84	16.51	13.83	15.21	12.59
	s	8.12	6.73	7.04	6.51	7.07
RCC	$\bar{X}$	23.86	26.18	23.02	22.66	20.65
	s	8.41	8.27	8.38	8.31	8.19

No answer: 8

Table III.9 *Criterion-related Item Analysis Data, Sweden, Boys and Girls, IEA/1A:9*

Boys, Grade 3

Answers		A	B	C	D	E
	n	34	145	40	13	188
	%	8	35	10	3	45
WKC	$\bar{X}$	9.54	16.30	11.21	10.02	12.94
	s	7.46	6.55	7.41	9.47	7.91
RCC	$\bar{X}$	10.12	23.85	16.83	15.47	19.01
	s	8.12	9.93	10.99	9.90	9.35

No answer: 2

Boys, Grade 4

Answers		A	B	C	D	E
	n	38	208	38	9	171
	%	8	45	8	2	37
WKC	$\bar{X}$	13.16	17.60	13.40	11.22	15.19
	s	7.85	7.48	6.93	7.93	7.47
RCC	$\bar{X}$	19.09	27.24	19.56	14.00	22.22
	s	11.06	9.33	9.40	9.45	9.53

No answer: 3

Girls, Grade 3

Answers		A	B	C	D	E
	n	25	118	26	19	217
	%	6	29	6	5	54
WKC	$\bar{X}$	11.16	16.21	10.00	10.91	11.84
	s	7.52	6.14	7.05	8.54	6.84
RCC	$\bar{X}$	14.68	24.70	17.83	15.81	19.80
	s	10.59	9.28	10.46	8.77	8.99

No answer: 3

Girls, Grade 4

Answers		A	B	C	D	E
	n	20	204	29	17	189
	%	4	44	6	4	41
WKC	$\bar{X}$	11.16	16.42	13.83	13.88	14.64
	s	9.14	6.66	7.41	5.35	7.22
RCC	$\bar{X}$	21.53	26.79	20.03	19.27	23.52
	s	8.37	8.01	10.08	7.45	8.29

No answer: 3

Table III.10 *Criterion-related Item Analysis Data, Sweden, Boys and Girls, IEA/1A:10*

Boys, Grade 3

Answers		A	B	C	D	E
	n	47	44	23	282	24
	%	11	10	5	67	6
WKC	$\bar{X}$	11.33	12.48	13.83	14.19	13.05
	s	6.87	6.70	7.98	7.92	7.55
RCC	$\bar{X}$	13.19	18.93	17.48	21.41	14.56
	s	8.19	11.33	12.00	9.92	9.37

No answer: 2

Boys, Grade 4

Answers		A	B	C	D	E
	n	35	33	34	341	23
	%	8	7	7	73	5
WKC	$\bar{X}$	12.15	18.67	12.89	16.70	9.49
	s	6.94	5.62	8.53	7.42	7.05
RCC	$\bar{X}$	19.24	24.20	18.31	25.25	16.74
	s	10.28	10.93	8.98	9.66	9.60

No answer: 1

Girls, Grade 3

Answers		A	B	C	D	E
	n	38	34	23	282	25
	%	9	8	6	70	6
WKC	$\bar{X}$	9.92	11.18	8.28	13.89	12.56
	s	5.27	6.24	8.31	6.97	8.31
RCC	$\bar{X}$	15.92	16.95	14.52	22.29	18.10
	s	8.80	9.68	8.34	9.49	9.37

No answer: 6

Girls, Grade 4

Answers		A	B	C	D	E
	n	18	34	22	366	19
	%	4	7	5	80	4
WKC	$\bar{X}$	13.67	15.32	14.14	15.32	15.26
	s	6.29	5.21	6.84	7.41	6.31
RCC	$\bar{X}$	20.82	22.73	24.10	25.13	20.10
	s	8.86	7.52	8.18	8.54	8.61

No answer: 3

Table III.11 *Criterion-related Item Analysis Data, Sweden, Boys and Girls, IEA/1A:14*

Boys, Grade 3

Answers		A	B	C	D	E
	n	291	12	17	51	50
	%	69	3	4	12	12
WKC	$\bar{X}$	15.05	7.52	10.83	10.91	10.09
	s	7.14	9.27	6.76	8.64	7.36
RCC	$\bar{X}$	21.48	10.86	13.28	15.21	17.54
	s	9.89	7.92	9.69	9.69	11.10
No answer:		1				

Boys, Grade 4

Answers		A	B	C	D	E
	n	375	7	12	31	42
	%	80	2	3	7	9
WKC	$\bar{X}$	16.21	12.87	16.67	10.95	16.43
	s	7.67	7.64	4.12	7.60	7.02
RCC	$\bar{X}$	24.55	14.53	16.05	18.36	24.44
	s	10.04	9.87	8.69	9.21	9.40
No answer:		0				

Girls, Grade 3

Answers		A	B	C	D	E
	n	212	10	15	85	81
	%	53	2	4	21	20
WKC	$\bar{X}$	13.69	8.61	10.01	12.59	12.30
	s	6.93	7.59	7.61	7.12	7.01
RCC	$\bar{X}$	21.31	16.73	19.17	21.08	20.53
	s	9.57	6.44	10.72	9.34	10.27
No answer:		5				

Girls, Grade 4

Answers		A	B	C	D	E
	n	275	13	15	81	77
	%	60	3	3	18	17
WKC	$\bar{X}$	15.50	14.00	14.14	15.37	14.66
	s	6.98	5.34	8.76	7.02	7.30
RCC	$\bar{X}$	24.66	21.86	25.15	24.31	24.72
	s	8.57	10.19	6.40	7.98	8.81
No answer:		1				

Table III.12 *Criterion-related Item Analysis Data, Sweden, Boys and Girls, IEA/1A:16*

Boys, Grade 3

Answers		A	B	C	D	E
	n	17	24	57	287	35
	%	4	6	14	68	8
WKC	$\bar{X}$	9.13	10.17	12.94	14.62	10.69
	s	9.47	6.54	8.32	7.45	6.63
RCC	$\bar{X}$	14.36	13.97	18.64	21.08	16.05
	s	10.56	10.23	9.76	9.99	11.43

No answer: 2

Boys, Grade 4

Answers		A	B	C	D	E
	n	12	18	45	363	28
	%	3	4	10	78	6
WKC	$\bar{X}$	10.18	12.62	13.69	16.59	13.82
	s	6.66	9.72	7.65	7.32	8.43
RCC	$\bar{X}$	17.11	19.22	20.04	25.03	19.19
	s	9.85	9.44	11.13	9.64	11.12

No answer: 1

Girls, Grade 3

Answers		A	B	C	D	E
	n	15	27	69	223	65
	%	4	7	17	56	16
WKC	$\bar{X}$	9.08	9.90	13.57	13.98	11.30
	s	7.52	9.54	6.31	6.62	7.15
RCC	$\bar{X}$	15.64	19.54	19.97	22.12	18.22
	s	10.35	9.93	9.22	9.15	10.88

No answer: 9

Girls, Grade 4

Answers		A	B	C	D	E
	n	24	12	91	286	47
	%	5	3	20	62	10
WKC	$\bar{X}$	13.92	15.00	14.74	15.59	14.87
	s	8.39	5.91	7.73	6.90	6.28
RCC	$\bar{X}$	22.27	21.02	22.67	25.75	23.01
	s	8.88	9.87	8.95	7.89	9.37

No answer: 2

Table III.13 *Criterion-related Item Analysis Data, Sweden, Boys and Girls, IEA/1A:20*

Boys, Grade 3

Answers		A	B	C	D	E
	n	18	29	41	205	113
	%	4	7	10	50	28
WKC	$\bar{X}$	12.06	10.94	12.32	15.83	11.09
	s	7.49	9.17	7.58	6.94	7.70
RCC	$\bar{X}$	14.75	12.70	19.60	22.85	16.86
	s	13.46	9.21	9.03	9.73	9.91

No answer: 16

Boys, Grade 4

Answers		A	B	C	D	E
	n	14	19	49	302	79
	%	3	4	11	65	17
WKC	$\bar{X}$	13.65	13.79	13.50	17.31	12.79
	s	9.97	7.00	7.43	7.26	7.60
RCC	$\bar{X}$	17.10	14.64	21.26	26.23	19.99
	s	7.99	11.38	8.30	9.42	10.22

No answer: 4

Girls, Grade 3

Answers		A	B	C	D	E
	n	14	17	52	163	132
	%	4	5	14	43	35
WKC	$\bar{X}$	11.14	11.72	12.31	15.07	11.69
	s	6.85	8.22	7.46	6.85	6.64
RCC	$\bar{X}$	20.86	16.56	19.00	24.91	18.17
	s	9.47	7.79	10.12	8.73	8.98

No answer: 30

Girls, Grade 4

Answers		A	B	C	D	E
	n	29	24	53	229	117
	%	6	5	12	51	26
WKC	$\bar{X}$	14.11	13.00	15.49	16.33	13.85
	s	7.82	6.56	6.82	6.73	7.54
RCC	$\bar{X}$	22.54	21.22	23.03	27.20	21.45
	s	8.42	8.54	8.40	7.66	8.46

No answer: 10

Table III.14 *Criterion-related Item Analysis Data, Sweden, Boys and Girls, IEA/1B:10*

Boys, Grade 3

Answers		A	B	C	D	E
	n	76	150	73	34	65
	%	19	38	18	9	16
WKC	$\bar{X}$	12.91	14.76	13.76	11.22	12.81
	s	6.70	7.59	7.54	8.02	8.54
RCC	$\bar{X}$	19.15	22.27	18.98	14.94	17.32
	s	9.54	10.33	10.16	9.65	10.69
No answer:		24				

Girls, Grade 3

Answers		A	B	C	D	E
	n	65	175	53	26	61
	%	17	46	14	7	16
WKC	$\bar{X}$	11.88	14.21	11.55	11.12	12.19
	s	7.82	6.62	7.62	7.69	6.88
RCC	$\bar{X}$	19.58	23.38	18.27	14.54	18.65
	s	10.41	8.50	10.39	9.50	9.65
No answer:		28				

Boys, Grade 4

Answers		A	B	C	D	E
	n	78	199	85	40	55
	%	17	44	19	9	12
WKC	$\bar{X}$	15.78	17.57	14.06	13.78	13.79
	s	7.20	7.65	7.46	7.04	7.59
RCC	$\bar{X}$	22.81	27.86	20.55	18.84	18.49
	s	10.07	9.01	9.39	10.25	9.41
No answer:		10				

Girls, Grade 4

Answers		A	B	C	D	E
	n	69	221	66	29	61
	%	15	50	15	7	14
WKC	$\bar{X}$	14.83	16.78	13.76	13.21	12.40
	s	6.92	6.85	7.81	5.88	7.34
RCC	$\bar{X}$	23.36	27.14	22.63	21.74	19.75
	s	8.50	7.64	9.12	8.49	8.40
No answer:		16				

Scale Types and Coefficients for Low Achieving Students

Table IV.1 *Scale Types for Low Achieving Students*

GUTSC1C = 1A:9(2), 1A:16(2), 1B:10(2)
GUTSC2D = 1A:10(2), 1A:14(2), 1A:16(2)
GUTSC3A = 1A:8(2), 1A:16(2), 1A:20(2)
(Cutting points in brackets)

Scale type	GUTSC1C: Score pattern			Frequency			
	Items by difficulty a)			Sweden boys	Sweden girls	Sweden total	India boys
	1A:9	1B:10	1A:16				
3	2	2	2	4	4	8	7
2	1	2	2	24	27	51	51
1	1	1	2	28	43	71	73
0	1	1	1	10	14	24	26
				66	88	154	157

a) India, order of difficulty reversed: 1A:16, 1B:10, 1A:9

Scale type	GUTSC2D: Score pattern			Frequency			
	Items by difficulty b)			Sweden boys	Sweden girls	Sweden total	India boys
	1A:16	1A:10	1A:14				
3	2	2	2	2	3	5	15
2	1	2	2	7	16	23	35
1	1	1	2	9	9	18	43
0	1	1	1	2	2	4	17
				20	30	50	110

b) India, order of difficulty reversed: 1A:16, 1A:14, 1A:10

Scale type	GUTSC3A: Score pattern			Frequency			
	Items by difficulty c)			Sweden boys	Sweden girls	Sweden total	India boys
	1A:20	1A:16	1A:8				
3	2	2	2	1	2	3	1
2	1	2	2	22	20	42	42
1	1	1	2	20	41	61	67
0	1	1	1	17	18	35	57
				60	81	141	167

c) Sweden, girls, order of difficulty reversed: 1A:20, 1A:8, 1A:16

Table IV.2 *Coefficients for Scales Low Achieving Students*

1= Coefficient of reproducibility
2= Minimum marginal reproducibility
3= Percent improvement
4= Coefficient of scalability

Scale	Group	Coefficients			
		1	2	3	4
GUTSC1C	Sweden, boys	.727	.596	.131	.325
	Sweden, girls	.803	.640	.163	.453
	Sweden, total	.771	.621	.149	.394
	India, boys	.711	.612	.100	.257
GUTSC2D	Sweden, total[a]	.707	.567	.140	.323
	India, boys	.776	.624	.152	.403
GUTSC3A	Sweden, boys	.867	.661	.206	.607
	Sweden, girls	.844	.679	.165	.513
	Sweden, total	.844	.657	.187	.545
	India, boys	.844	.693	.152	.494

[a] Separate scaling of Sweden, boys and Sweden, girls, was not possible due to low number of low achieving students on the items of this scale

Scale Types and Coefficients for Ten Guttman-Scales

Table V.1 *Scale Types based on Items IEA/1A:9, IEA/1A:16, IEA/1B:10*

GUTSC1A = 1A:9(2), 1A:16(2), 1B:10(3)

GUTSC1B = 1A:9(3), 1A:16(2), 1B:10(3)

(Cutting points in brackets)

Scale type	GUTSC1A: Score pattern			Frequency			
	Items by difficulty			Sweden boys	Sweden girls	Sweden total	India boys
	1B:10	1A:9	1A:16				
3	3	2,3	2,3	181	179	360	144
2	2,1	2,3	2,3	377	301	678	289
1	2,1	1	2,3	211	202	413	223
0	2,1	1	1	21	30	51	50
				790	712	1502	706

Scale type	GUTSC1B: Score pattern			Frequency			
	Items by difficulty x)			Sweden boys	Sweden girls	Sweden total	India boys
	1B:10	1A:9	1A:16				
3	3	3	2,3	132	140	272	102
2	2,1	3	2,3	356	304	660	248
1	2,1	2,1	2,3	273	231	504	250
0	2,1	2,1	1	29	37	66	106
				790	712	1502	706

x) Sweden, order of difficulty reversed: 1A:9, 1B:10, 1A:16.

Table V.2 *Coefficients for Scales based on IEA/1A:9, IEA/1A:16, IEA/1B:10*

1 = Coefficient of reproducibility
2 = Minimum marginal reproducibility
3 = Percent improvement
4 = Coefficient of scalability

Scale	Group	Coefficients			
		1	2	3	4
GUTSC1A	Sweden, boys	.857	.690	.166	.537
	Sweden, girls	.832	.641	.192	.533
	Sweden, total	.845	.667	.178	.535
	India, boys	.810	.680	.130	.406
GUTSC1B	Sweden, boys	.821	.693	.128	.417
	Sweden, girls	.851	.673	.178	.545
	Sweden, total	.835	.684	.152	.480
	India, boys	.823	.646	.178	.501

Table V.3 *Scale Types based on Items IEA/1A:10, IEA/1A:14, IEA/1A:16*

GUTSC2A = 1A:10(2), 1A:14(3), 1A:16(2)

GUTSC2B = 1A:10(3), 1A:14(3), 1A:16(2)

GUTSC2C = 1A:10(2), 1A:14(3), 1A:16(3)

GUTSC2E = 1A:10(2), 1A:14(2), 1A:16(3)

(Cutting points in brackets)

Scale type	GUTSC2A: Score pattern			Frequency			
	Items by difficulty x)			Sweden boys	Sweden girls	Sweden total	India boys
	1A:14	1A:10	1A:16				
3	3	2,3	2,3	514	344	858	189
2	2,1	2,3	2,3	237	319	556	342
1	2,1	1	2,3	59	70	129	146
0	2,1	1	1	9	6	15	38
				819	739	1558	715

x) India, order of difficulty reversed: 1A:14, 1A:16, 1A:10

Scale type	GUTSC2B: Score pattern			Frequency			
	Items by difficulty			Sweden boys	Sweden girls	Sweden total	India boys
	1A:14	1A:10	1A:16				
3	3	3	3,2	430	293	723	161
2	1,2	3	3,2	291	329	620	311
1	1,2	1,2	3,2	83	104	187	164
0	1,2	1,2	1	15	13	28	79
				819	739	1558	715

Scale type	GUTSC2C: Score pattern			Frequency			
	Items by difficulty			Sweden boys	Sweden girls	Sweden total	India boys
	1A:14	1A:16	1A:10				
3	3	3	3,2	452	268	720	153
2	1,2	3	3,2	262	322	584	293
1	1,2	1,2	3,2	95	134	229	224
0	1,2	1,2	1	10	15	25	45
				819	739	1558	715

Table V.3 *Scale Types based on Items IEA/1A:10, IEA/1A:14, IEA/1A:16 (continued)*

Scale type	GUTSC2E: Score pattern			Frequency			
	Items by difficulty			Sweden boys	Sweden girls	Sweden total	India boys
	1A:16	1A:14	1A:10				
3	3	2,3	2,3	511	376	887	227
2	1,2	2,3	2,3	246	285	531	349
1	1,2	1	2,3	60	74	134	117
0	1,2	1	1	2	4	6	22
				819	739	1558	715

Table V.4 *Coefficients for Scales based on IEA/1A:10, IEA/1A:14, IEA/1A:16*

1 = Coefficient of reproducibility
2 = Minimum marginal reproducibility
3 = Percent improvement
4 = Coefficient of scalability

Scale	Group	Coefficients			
		1	2	3	4
GUTSC2A	Sweden, boys	.893	.845	.049	.314
	Sweden, girls	.895	.785	.110	.509
	Sweden, total	.894	.816	.078	.423
	India, boys	.905	.739	.166	.635
GUTSC2B	Sweden, boys	.862	.796	.067	.327
	Sweden, girls	.855	.740	.115	.441
	Sweden, total	.842	.769	.072	.314
	India, boys	.842	.680	.163	.508
GUTSC2C	Sweden, boys	.840	.804	.036	.183
	Sweden, girls	.839	.714	.125	.436
	Sweden, total	.839	.761	.078	.327
	India, boys	.878	.680	.198	.619
GUTSC2E	Sweden, boys	.871	.849	.023	.151
	Sweden, girls	.866	.799	.066	.330
	Sweden, total	.866	.825	.041	.234
	India, boys	.824	.697	.126	.418

Table V.5 *Scale Types based on Items IEA/1A:8, IEA/1A:16, IEA/1A:20*

GUTSC3A = 1A:20(2), 1A:8(2), 1A:16(2)

GUTSC3B = 1A:8(3), 1A:16(2), 1A:20(2)

GUTSC3C = 1A:8(2), 1A:16(2), 1A:20(3)

GUTSC3D = 1A:8(3), 1A:16(2), 1A:20(3)

(Cutting points in brackets)

Scale type	GUTSC3A: Score pattern			Frequency			
	Items by difficulty			Sweden boys	Sweden girls	Sweden total	India boys
	1A:20	1A:8	1A:16				
3	3,2	3,2	3,2	349	253	602	105
2	1	3,2	3,2	322	322	644	360
1	1	1	3,2	103	111	214	170
0	1	1	1	17	18	35	56
				791	704	1495	691

Scale type	GUTSC3B: Score pattern			Frequency			
	Items by difficulty			Sweden boys	Sweden girls	Sweden total	India boys
	1A:8	1A:20	1A:16				
3	3	3,2	3,2	267	190	457	50
2	1,2	3,2	3,2	331	317	648	242
1	1,2	1	3,2	165	165	330	306
0	1,2	1	1	28	32	60	93
				791	704	1495	691

Scale type	GUTSC3C: Score pattern			Frequency			
	Items by difficulty			Sweden boys	Sweden girls	Sweden total	India boys
	1A:20	1A:8	1A:16				
3	3	3,2	3,2	331	227	558	78
2	1,2	3,2	3,2	329	343	672	367
1	1,2	1	3,2	114	113	227	183
0	1,2	1	1	17	21	38	63
				791	704	1495	691

Table V.5 *Scale Types based on Items IEA/1A:8, IEA/1A:16, IEA/1A:20 (continued)*

Scale type	GUTSC3D: Score pattern			Frequency			
	Items by difficulty			Sweden boys	Sweden girls	Sweden total	India boys
	1A:8	1A:20	1A:16				
3	3	3	3,2	256	173	429	40
2	1,2	3	3,2	326	321	647	219
1	1,2	1,2	3,2	179	174	353	328
0	1,2	1,2	1	30	36	66	104
				791	704	1495	691

Table V.6 *Coefficients for Scales based on IEA/1A:8, IEA/1A:16, IEA/1A:20*

1 = Coefficient of reproducibility
2 = Minimum marginal reproducibility
3 = Percent improvement
4 = Coefficient of scalability

Scale	Group	Coefficients			
		1	2	3	4
GUTSC3A	Sweden, boys	.853	.756	.097	.396
	Sweden, girls	.855	.717	.138	.488
	Sweden, total	.854	.738	.116	.443
	India, boys	.800	.690	.111	.356
GUTSC3B	Sweden, boys	.873	.686	.187	.595
	Sweden, girls	.822	.648	.174	.494
	Sweden, total	.849	.668	.181	.544
	India, boys	.808	.689	.119	.383
GUTSC3C	Sweden, boys	.858	.744	.115	.447
	Sweden, girls	.861	.710	.151	.520
	Sweden, total	.860	.724	.136	.492
	India, boys	.815	.716	.099	.348
GUTSC3D	Sweden, boys	.865	.674	.191	.587
	Sweden, girls	.824	.642	.182	.509
	Sweden, total	.839	.654	.185	.535
	India, boys	.818	.715	.103	.360

Correlation Coefficients

Table VI.1 *Spearman Correlation Coefficients for Ten Guttman Scales, Sweden, Boys* (N = 770 - 819)[a]

	GUTSC1A	GUTSC1B	GUTSC2A	GUTSC2B	GUTSC2C	GUTSC2E	GUTSC3A	GUTSC3B	GUTSC3C	GUTSC3D
GUTSC1A	1.0	.88	.16	.18	.14	.14	.22	.27	.21	.26
GUTSC1B		1.0	.20	.21	.19	.19	.27	.32	.26	.31
GUTSC2A			1.0	.85	.88	.72	.30	.33	.30	.33
GUTSC2B				1.0	.76	.61	.31	.34	.32	.35
GUTSC2C					1.0	.89	.27	.34	.28	.35
GUTSC2E						1.0	.23	.31	.24	.31
GUTSC3A							1.0	.86	.97	.83
GUTSC3B								1.0	.84	.97
GUTSC3C									1.0	.87
GUTSC3D										1.0

[a] Correlations involving GUTSC1A-B: N = 790
Correlations involving GUTSC2A-E: N = 819
Correlations involving GUTSC3A-D: N = 791
Correlations involving GUTSC1A-B x GUTSC2A-E: N = 788
Correlations involving GUTSC1A-B x GUTSC3A-D: N = 770
Correlations involving GUTSC2A-E x GUTSC3A-D: N = 788

Table VI.2 *Spearman Correlation Coefficients for Ten Guttman Scales, Sweden, Girls (N = 678 -739)*[a]

	GUTSC1A	GUTSC1B	GUTSC2A	GUTSC2B	GUTSC2C	GUTSC2E	GUTSC3A	GUTSC3B	GUTSC3C	GUTSC3D
GUTSC1A	1.0	.92	.28	.29	.23	.23	.27	.27	.27	.26
GUTSC1B		1.0	.30	.30	.26	.26	.29	.31	.29	.30
GUTSC2A			1.0	.89	.85	.59	.19	.21	.19	.21
GUTSC2B				1.0	.77	.53	.20	.22	.21	.23
GUTSC2C					1.0	.82	.19	.22	.19	.22
GUTSC2E						1.0	.21	.26	.21	.26
GUTSC3A							1.0	.87	.95	.82
GUTSC3B								1.0	.84	.96
GUTSC3C									1.0	.87
GUTSC3D										1.0

[a] Correlations involving GUTSC1A-B: N = 712
Correlations involving GUTSC2A-E: N = 739
Correlations involving GUTSC3A-D: N = 704
Correlations involving GUTSC1A-B x GUTSC2A-E: N = 708
Correlations involving GUTSC1A-B x GUTSC3A-D: N = 678
Correlations involving GUTSC2A-E x GUTSC3A-E: N = 699

Table VI.3 *Spearman Correlation Coefficients for Ten Guttman Scales, India, Boys* (N = 673 - 715)[a]

	GUTSC1A	GUTSC1B	GUTSC2A	GUTSC2B	GUTSC2C	GUTSC2E	GUTSC3A	GUTSC3B	GUTSC3C	GUTSC3D
GUTSC1A	1.0	.88	.48	.47	.40	.41	.43	.39	.45	.41
GUTSC1B		1.0	.51	.53	.45	.44	.47	.43	.50	.46
GUTSC2A			1.0	.91	.88	.74	.44	.39	.46	.40
GUTSC2B				1.0	.83	.68	.45	.39	.48	.41
GUTSC2C					1.0	.83	.37	.30	.39	.31
GUTSC2E						1.0	.36	.32	.38	.33
GUTSC3A							1.0	.80	.94	.73
GUTSC3B								1.0	.73	.94
GUTSC3C									1.0	.79
GUTSC3D										1.0

[a] Correlations involving GUTSC1A-B: N = 706
Correlations involving GUTSC2A-E: N = 715
Correlations involving GUTSC3A-D: N = 691
Correlations involving GUTSC1A-B x GUTSC2A-E: N = 689
Correlations involving GUTSC1A-B x GUTSC3A-D: N = 673
Correlations involving GUTSC2A-E x GUTSC3A-D: N = 677

Table VI.4 *Eta Correlation Coefficients for Ten Guttman Scales (IV) and Six Tests (DV), Sweden, Boys*
(Eta^2 are given in brackets)
(N = 790 - 819)[a]

	GUTSC1A	GUTSC1B	GUTSC2A	GUTSC2B	GUTSC2C	GUTSC2E	GUTSC3A	GUTSC3B	GUTSC3C	GUTSC3D
THINKING	.70 (.49)	.74 (.55)	.68 (.46)	.67 (.46)	.66 (.43)	.59 (.35)	.74 (.54)	.79 (.63)	.74 (.55)	.79 (.63)
RL	.63 (.39)	.67 (.45)	.54 (.30)	.58 (.34)	.56 (.32)	.51 (.26)	.68 (.47)	.75 (.56)	.69 (.47)	.75 (.56)
WKC	.24 (.06)	.32 (.10)	.29 (.08)	.27 (.07)	.29 (.09)	.25 (.06)	.25 (.06)	.31 (.10)	.26 (.07)	.31 (.10)
RCC	.34 (.11)	.45 (.20)	.33 (.11)	.33 (.11)	.35 (.12)	.28 (.08)	.32 (.10)	.41 (.17)	.34 (.12)	.34 (.12)
SCAB	.42 (.17)	.52 (.27)	.45 (.20)	.46 (.21)	.47 (.22)	.42 (.18)	.46 (.21)	.58 (.33)	.48 (.23)	.60 (.36)
SCABMIN	.32 (.10)	.42 (.17)	.37 (.14)	.35 (.12)	.37 (.14)	.34 (.12)	.36 (.13)	.46 (.21)	.38 (.15)	.48 (.23)

[a] Correlations involving THINKING x GUTSC1A-B: N = 790
Correlations involving RL, WKC, RCC, SCAB, SCABMIN x GUTSC1A-B: N = 790

Correlations involving THINKING x GUTSC2A-E: N = 808
Correlations involving RL, WKC, RCC, SCAB, SCABMIN x GUTSC2A-E: N = 819

Correlations involving THINKING x GUTSC3A-D: N = 790
Correlations involving RL, WKC, RCC, SCAB, SCABMIN x GUTSC3A-D: N = 791

Table VI.5 *Eta Correlation Coefficients for Ten Guttman Scales (IV) and Six Tests (DV), Sweden, Girls*
(Eta^2 are given in brackets)
(N = 701 - 739)[a]

	GUTSC1A	GUTSC1B	GUTSC2A	GUTSC2B	GUTSC2C	GUTSC2E	GUTSC3A	GUTSC3B	GUTSC3C	GUTSC3D
THINKING	.78 (.61)	.81 (.65)	.68 (.47)	.66 (.43)	.63 (.39)	.59 (.34)	.72 (.52)	.75 (.57)	.72 (.52)	.75 (.57)
RL	.69 (.48)	.71 (.50)	.53 (.28)	.55 (.31)	.55 (.30)	.54 (.29)	.64 (.41)	.67 (.45)	.64 (.40)	.66 (.43)
WKC	.25 (.06)	.30 (.09)	.17 (.03)	.21 (.05)	.16 (.02)	.13 (.02)	.21 (.04)	.24 (.06)	.22 (.05)	.26 (.07)
RCC	.30 (.09)	.36 (.13)	.18 (.03)	.21 (.05)	.20 (.04)	.18 (.03)	.33 (.11)	.39 (.15)	.33 (.11)	.39 (.15)
SCAB	.46 (.21)	.52 (.27)	.35 (.12)	.40 (.16)	.39 (.15)	.38 (.14)	.42 (.18)	.51 (.26)	.44 (.19)	.52 (.27)
SCABMIN	.34 (.12)	.39 (.15)	.23 (.05)	.27 (.07)	.24 (.06)	.26 (.07)	.33 (.11)	.40 (.16)	.33 (.11)	.40 (.16)

[a] Correlations involving THINKING x GUTSC1A-B: N = 710
Correlations involving RL, WKC, RCC, SCAB, SCABMIN x GUTSC1A-B: N = 739

Correlations involving THINKING x GUTSC2A-E: N = 731
Correlations involving RL, WKC, RCC, SCAB, SCABMIN x GUTSC2A-E: N = 739

Correlations involving THINKING x GUTSC3A-D: N = 701
Correlations involving RL, WKC, RCC, SCAB, SCABMIN x GUTSC3A-D: N = 704

Table VI.6 *Eta Correlation Coefficients for Ten Guttman Scales (IV) and Six Tests (DV), India, Boys*
(Eta^2 are given in brackets)
(N = 690 - 715)[a]

	GUTSC1A	GUTSC1B	GUTSC2A	GUTSC2B	GUTSC2C	GUTSC2E	GUTSC3A	GUTSC3B	GUTSC3C	GUTSC3D
THINKING	.81 (.65)	.86 (.74)	.81 (.65)	.79 (.63)	.72 (.52)	.69 (.48)	.77 (.59)	.75 (.56)	.78 (.61)	.76 (.58)
RL	.70 (.49)	.75 (.56)	.65 (.42)	.69 (.47)	.65 (.42)	.66 (.43)	.65 (.42)	.65 (.43)	.65 (.42)	.65 (.43)
WKC	.32 (.10)	.36 (.13)	.38 (.15)	.43 (.18)	.35 (.12)	.25 (.07)	.31 (.10)	.27 (.07)	.32 (.10)	.27 (.07)
RCC	.19 (.04)	.29 (.09)	.29 (.08)	.34 (.12)	.29 (.09)	.18 (.03)	.26 (.07)	.20 (.04)	.28 (.08)	.20 (.04)
SCAB	.47 (.22)	.58 (.34)	.50 (.25)	.57 (.32)	.50 (.25)	.41 (.17)	.36 (.13)	.43 (.18)	.40 (.16)	.48 (.23)
SCABMIN	.37 (.13)	.46 (.21)	.40 (.16)	.46 (.21)	.39 (.15)	.31 (.10)	.26 (.07)	.32 (.10)	.30 (.09)	.36 (.13)

[a] Correlations involving THINKING x GUTSC1A-B: N = 702
Correlations involving RL, WKC, RCC, SCAB, SCABMIN x GUTSC1A-B: N = 706

Correlations involving THINKING x GUTSC2A-E: N = 706
Correlations involving RL, WKC, RCC, SCAB, SCABMIN x GUTSC2A-E: N = 715

Correlations involving THINKING x GUTSC3A-D: N = 690
Correlations involving RL, WKC, RCC, SCAB, SCABMIN x GUTSC3A-D: N = 691

Table VI.7 *Pearson Correlation Coefficients for Six Tests, Sweden, Boys*

Variable	X_1	X_2	X_3	X_4	X_5	X_6
X_1 Thinking		.90	.39	.51	.68	.54
X_2 Reasoning Level			.39	.53	.70	.54
X_3 Word Knowledge				.54	.51	.49
X_4 Reading Comprehension					.69	.66
X_5 Science I						.97
X_6 Science Minimized						

Table VI.8 *Pearson Correlation Coefficients for Six Tests, Sweden, Girls*

Variable	X_1	X_2	X_3	X_4	X_5	X_6
X_1 Thinking		.88	.31	.41	.62	.45
X_2 Reasoning Level			.33	.46	.68	.51
X_3 Word Knowledge				.51	.52	.51
X_4 Reading Comprehension					.69	.67
X_5 Science I						.97
X_6 Science Minimized						

Table VI.9 *Pearson Correlation Coefficients for Six Tests, India, Boys*

Variable	X_1	X_2	X_3	X_4	X_5	X_6
X_1 Thinking		.87	.41	.32	.61	.47
X_2 Reasoning Level			.42	.33	.64	.49
X_3 Word Knowledge				.53	.55	.53
X_4 Reading Comprehension					.51	.49
X_5 Science I						.98
X_6 Science Minimized						

Appendix VII

Analyses of Variances and Tests of Linearity of Ten Guttman Scales

(Sample and Dependent Variable are given in Table Headings)

Table VII.1 *Sweden, Boys - Science Total Corrected Score*

Guttman scale	Scale types 0	1	2	3	Analysis of variance	Test of linearity
GUTSC1A	N= 21	N= 211	N= 377	N= 161	F= 55.47	F= .33
	X̄=12.19	X̄=17.00	X̄=20.49	X̄=24.39	df= 3, 786	df= 2, 786
	s= 6.16	s= 5.98	s= 6.32	s= 6.85	p < .01	NS
GUTSC1B	N= 29	N= 273	N= 356	N= 132	F= 99.18	F= .25
	X̄=12.08	X̄=16.77	X̄=21.26	X̄=26.38	df= 3, 786	df= 2, 786
	s= 5.57	s= 5.97	s= 6.03	s= 5.81	p < .01	NS
GUTSC2A	N= 9	N= 59	N= 237	N= 514	F= 69.07	F= 2.14
	X̄= 8.52	X̄=14.24	X̄=17.10	X̄=22.40	df= 3, 815	df= 2, 815
	s= 8.19	s= 4.91	s= 5.94	s= 6.48	p < .01	NS
GUTSC2B	N= 15	N= 83	N= 291	N= 430	F= 72.89	F= .37
	X̄=10.29	X̄=14.40	X̄=18.22	X̄=22.86	df= 3, 815	df= 2, 815
	s= 6.84	s= 5.62	s= 6.22	s= 6.29	p < .01	NS
GUTSC2C	N= 10	N= 95	N= 262	N= 452	F= 78.73	F= 1.92
	X̄= 9.42	X̄=14.63	X̄=17.75	X̄=22.89	df= 3, 815	df= 2, 815
	s= 8.23	s= 5.56	s= 5.98	s= 6.33	p < .01	NS
GUTSC2E	N= 2	N= 60	N= 246	N= 511	F= 58.49	F= 2.57
	X̄= 3.05	X̄=14.34	X̄=17.20	X̄=22.28	df= 3, 815	df= 2, 815
	s= 1.06	s= 6.90	s= 5.96	s= 6.46	p < .01	NS
GUTSC3A	N= 17	N= 103	N= 322	N= 349	F= 69.28	F= 1.93
	X̄=12.31	X̄=15.36	X̄=18.64	X̄=23.54	df= 3, 787	df= 2, 787
	s= 4.96	s= 5.55	s= 6.10	s= 6.64	p < .01	NS
GUTSC3B	N= 28	N= 165	N= 331	N= 267	F= 130.46	F= 3.64
	X̄=11.60	X̄=15.39	X̄=19.34	X̄=25.25	df= 3, 787	df= 2, 787
	s= 5.45	s= 5.12	s= 5.99	s= 5.84	p < .01	p <.05
GUTSC3C	N= 17	N= 114	N= 329	N= 331	F= 80.35	F= 1.89
	X̄=12.31	X̄=15.06	X̄=18.80	X̄=23.86	df= 3, 787	df= 2, 787
	s= 4.96	s= 5.61	s= 6.05	s= 6.49	p < .01	NS
GUTSC3D	N= 30	N= 179	N= 326	N= 256	F= 144.70	F= 2.50
	X̄=11.42	X̄=15.29	X̄=19.65	X̄=25.48	df= 3, 787	df= 2, 787
	s= 5.47	s= 5.14	s= 5.88	s= 5.71	p < .01	NS

Table VII.2 *Sweden, Boys - Word Knowledge Total Corrected Score*

Guttman scale	Scale types 0	1	2	3	Analysis of variance	Test of linearity
GUTSC1A	N= 21	N= 211	N= 377	N= 181	F= 15.49	F= .88
	$\bar{X}$= 9.44	$\bar{X}$=13.35	$\bar{X}$=14.99	$\bar{X}$=17.78	df= 3, 786	df= 2, 786
	s= 7.63	s= 7.59	s= 7.48	s= 7.44	$p < .01$	NS
GUTSC1B	N= 29	N= 273	N= 356	N= 132	F= 29.32	F= 1.58
	$\bar{X}$= 9.25	$\bar{X}$=13.08	$\bar{X}$=15.35	$\bar{X}$=19.54	df= 3, 786	df= 2, 786
	s= 7.30	s= 7.57	s= 7.44	s= 6.47	$p < .01$	NS
GUTSC2A	N= 9	N= 59	N= 237	N= 514	F= 24.10	F= .50
	$\bar{X}$= 5.12	$\bar{X}$=10.71	$\bar{X}$=13.15	$\bar{X}$=16.53	df= 3, 815	df= 2, 815
	s= 6.57	s= 7.61	s= 7.69	s= 7.27	$p < .01$	NS
GUTSC2B	N= 15	N= 83	N= 291	N= 430	F= 21.68	F= .47
	$\bar{X}$= 9.94	$\bar{X}$=10.77	$\bar{X}$=13.86	$\bar{X}$=16.78	df= 3, 815	df= 2, 815
	s= 8.49	s= 7.23	s= 7.86	s= 7.15	$p < .01$	NS
GUTSC2C	N= 10	N= 95	N= 262	N= 452	F= 25.70	F= .36
	$\bar{X}$= 6.11	$\bar{X}$=11.08	$\bar{X}$=13.65	$\bar{X}$=16.81	df= 3, 815	df= 2, 815
	s= 6.94	s= 7.78	s= 7.68	s= 7.15	$p < .01$	NS
GUTSC2E	N= 2	N= 60	N= 246	N= 511	F= 17.85	F= .31
	$\bar{X}$= 3.50	$\bar{X}$=10.66	$\bar{X}$=13.35	$\bar{X}$=16.36	df= 3, 815	df= 2, 815
	s= 4.95	s= 7.39	s= 7.75	s= 7.39	$p < .01$	NS
GUTSC3A	N= 17	N= 103	N= 322	N= 349	F= 18.13	F= .92
	$\bar{X}$=11.54	$\bar{X}$=11.60	$\bar{X}$=14.24	$\bar{X}$=17.04	df= 3, 787	df= 2, 787
	s= 8.55	s= 7.25	s= 7.78	s= 7.16	$p < .01$	NS
GUTSC3B	N= 28	N= 165	N= 331	N= 267	F= 27.73	F= 1.89
	$\bar{X}$=10.83	$\bar{X}$=12.23	$\bar{X}$=14.39	$\bar{X}$=18.12	df= 3, 787	df= 2, 787
	s= 8.74	s= 7.47	s= 7.42	s= 6.98	$p < .01$	NS
GUTSC3C	N= 17	N= 114	N= 329	N= 331	F= 19.49	F= 1.07
	$\bar{X}$=11.54	$\bar{X}$=11.36	$\bar{X}$=14.51	$\bar{X}$=17.09	df= 3, 787	df= 2, 787
	s= 8.55	s= 7.34	s= 7.73	s= 7.12	$p < .01$	NS
GUTSC3D	N= 30	N= 179	N= 326	N= 256	F= 28.24	F= 1.07
	$\bar{X}$=10.24	$\bar{X}$=12.35	$\bar{X}$=14.58	$\bar{X}$=18.16	df= 3, 787	df= 2, 787
	s= 8.74	s= 7.40	s= 7.47	s= 6.90	$p < .01$	NS

Table VII.3 *Sweden, Boys - Reading Comprehension Total Corrected Score*

Guttman scale	Scale types 0	1	2	3	Analysis of variance	Test of linearity
GUTSC1A	N= 21	N= 211	N= 377	N= 181	F= 33.54	F= 1.66
	X̄=12.81	X̄=18.91	X̄=22.06	X̄=27.65	df= 3, 786	df= 2, 786
	s= 8.86	s= 9.38	s= 9.87	s= 9.89	p <.01	NS
GUTSC1B	N= 29	N= 273	N= 356	N= 132	F= 65.12	F= 2.26
	X̄=12.10	X̄=18.32	X̄=23.00	X̄=30.63	df= 3, 786	df= 2, 786
	s= 9.04	s= 9.49	s= 9.62	s= 7.53	p <.01	NS
GUTSC2A	N= 9	N= 59	N= 237	N= 514	F= 34.14	F= .75
	X̄= 8.60	X̄=15.63	X̄=19.05	X̄=24.65	df= 3, 815	df= 2, 815
	s= 5.84	s=10.97	s= 9.25	s= 9.81	p <.01	NS
GUTSC2B	N= 15	N= 83	N= 291	N= 430	F= 34.12	F= .15
	X̄=12.19	X̄=15.42	X̄=20.47	X̄=25.04	df= 3, 815	df= 2, 815
	s= 8.64	s=10.59	s= 9.56	s= 9.67	p <.01	NS
GUTSC2C	N= 10	N= 95	N= 262	N= 452	F= 38.27	F= 1.33
	X̄= 8.11	X̄=16.48	X̄=19.71	X̄=25.16	df= 3, 815	df= 2, 815
	s= 5.72	s=10.08	s= 9.78	s= 9.53	p <.01	NS
GUTSC2E	N= 2	N= 60	N= 246	N= 511	F= 23.25	F= 1.04
	X̄= 5.20	X̄=16.53	X̄=19.33	X̄=24.32	df= 3, 815	df= 2, 815
	s= 3.54	s=10.33	s=10.01	s= 9.78	p <.01	NS
GUTSC3A	N= 17	N= 103	N= 322	N= 349	F= 30.20	F= .40
	X̄=13.86	X̄=17.22	X̄=20.93	X̄=25.73	df= 3, 787	df= 2, 787
	s= 9.57	s= 9.99	s= 9.69	s= 9.66	p <.01	NS
GUTSC3B	N= 28	N= 165	N= 331	N= 267	F= 51.92	F= .93
	X̄=13.20	X̄=17.36	X̄=21.62	X̄=27.49	df= 3, 787	df= 2, 787
	s= 9.82	s= 9.36	s= 9.55	s= 9.12	p <.01	NS
GUTSC3C	N= 17	N= 114	N= 329	N= 331	F= 35.05	F= .31
	X̄=13.86	X̄=16.47	X̄=21.36	X̄=25.95	df= 3, 787	df= 2, 787
	s= 9.57	s=10.05	s= 9.54	s= 9.60	p <.01	NS
GUTSC3D	N= 30	N= 179	N= 326	N= 256	F= 57.10	F= .26
	X̄=12.65	X̄=17.20	X̄=22.05	X̄=27.66	df= 3, 787	df= 2, 787
	s= 9.73	s= 9.40	s= 9.39	s= 9.06	p <.01	NS

Table VII.4 *Sweden, Girls - Science Total Corrected Score*

Guttman scale	Scale types				Analysis of variance	Test of linearity
	0	1	2	3		
GUTSC1A	N= 30	N= 202	N= 301	N= 179	F= 63.86	F= 2.84
	$\bar{X}$= 9.34	$\bar{X}$=15.54	$\bar{X}$=18.73	$\bar{X}$=22.02	df= 3, 708	df= 2, 708
	s= 5.59	s= 5.64	s= 5.88	s= 5.93	$p < .01$	NS
GUTSC1B	N= 37	N= 231	N= 304	N= 140	F= 87.54	F= 1.62
	$\bar{X}$= 9.60	$\bar{X}$=15.38	$\bar{X}$=19.28	$\bar{X}$=23.06	df= 3, 708	df= 2, 708
	s= 5.27	s= 5.70	s= 5.64	s= 5.43	$p < .01$	NS
GUTSC2A	N= 6	N= 70	N= 319	N= 344	F= 33.20	F= 2.32
	$\bar{X}$= 5.83	$\bar{X}$=13.73	$\bar{X}$=17.29	$\bar{X}$=20.03	df= 3, 735	df= 2, 735
	s= 3.68	s= 6.08	s= 6.27	s= 6.02	$p < .01$	NS
GUTSC2B	N= 13	N= 104	N= 329	N= 293	F= 47.54	F= 2.56
	$\bar{X}$= 7.09	$\bar{X}$=14.29	$\bar{X}$=17.56	$\bar{X}$=20.65	df= 3, 735	df= 2, 735
	s= 5.10	s= 5.87	s= 6.12	s= 5.86	$p < .01$	NS
GUTSC2C	N= 15	N= 134	N= 322	N= 268	F= 42.97	F= .41
	$\bar{X}$=10.15	$\bar{X}$=14.47	$\bar{X}$=17.84	$\bar{X}$=20.78	df= 3, 735	df= 2, 735
	s= 6.32	s= 5.90	s= 6.34	s= 5.66	$p < .01$	NS
GUTSC2E	N= 4	N= 74	N= 285	N= 376	F= 40.82	F= .33
	$\bar{X}$= 7.23	$\bar{X}$=13.27	$\bar{X}$=16.75	$\bar{X}$=20.26	df= 3, 735	df= 2, 735
	s= 4.50	s= 6.26	s= 6.31	s= 5.79	$p < .01$	NS
GUTSC3A	N= 18	N= 111	N= 322	N= 253	F= 51.29	F= .26
	$\bar{X}$=10.86	$\bar{X}$=13.93	$\bar{X}$=17.93	$\bar{X}$=21.26	df= 3, 700	df= 2, 700
	s= 5.24	s= 5.62	s= 6.11	s= 5.80	$p < .01$	NS
GUTSC3B	N= 32	N= 165	N= 317	N= 190	F= 83.10	F= .56
	$\bar{X}$=10.05	$\bar{X}$=14.41	$\bar{X}$=18.77	$\bar{X}$=22.33	df= 3, 700	df= 2, 700
	s= 5.50	s= 5.32	s= 5.83	s= 5.46	$p < .01$	NS
GUTSC3C	N= 21	N= 113	N= 343	N= 227	F= 55.92	F= .21
	$\bar{X}$=11.21	$\bar{X}$=14.06	$\bar{X}$=17.91	$\bar{X}$=21.69	df= 3, 700	df= 2, 700
	s= 5.06	s= 5.65	s= 6.06	s= 5.71	$p < .01$	NS
GUTSC3D	N= 36	N= 174	N= 321	N= 173	F= 87.83	F= .17
	$\bar{X}$=10.32	$\bar{X}$=14.58	$\bar{X}$=18.87	$\bar{X}$=22.70	df= 3, 700	df= 2, 700
	s= 5.34	s= 5.25	s= 5.87	s= 5.30	$p < .01$	NS

Table VII.5 *Sweden, Girls - Word Knowledge Total Corrected Score*

Guttman scale	Scale types 0	1	2	3	Analysis of variance	Test of linearity
GUTSC1A	N= 30	N= 202	N= 301	N= 179	F= 15.90	F= .16
	$\bar{X}$=10.61	$\bar{X}$=12.57	$\bar{X}$=14.51	$\bar{X}$=17.00	df= 3, 708	df= 2, 708
	s= 7.98	s= 7.40	s= 6.77	s= 6.65	p <.01	NS
GUTSC1B	N= 37	N= 231	N= 304	N= 140	F= 23.85	F= .38
	$\bar{X}$= 9.63	$\bar{X}$=12.59	$\bar{X}$=14.79	$\bar{X}$=17.92	df= 3, 708	df= 2, 708
	s= 7.97	s= 7.42	s= 6.49	s= 6.40	p <.01	NS
GUTSC2A	N= 6	N= 70	N= 319	N= 344	F= 7.61	F= 2.41
	$\bar{X}$= 5.68	$\bar{X}$=11.82	$\bar{X}$=14.28	$\bar{X}$=15.19	df= 3, 735	df= 2, 735
	s= 5.43	s= 7.32	s= 7.27	s= 6.87	p <.01	NS
GUTSC2B	N= 13	N= 104	N= 329	N= 293	F= 11.58	F= 5.15
	$\bar{X}$= 5.01	$\bar{X}$=12.76	$\bar{X}$=14.41	$\bar{X}$=15.40	df= 3, 735	df= 2, 735
	s= 6.59	s= 6.73	s= 7.21	s= 6.93	p <.01	p <.01
GUTSC2C	N= 15	N= 134	N= 322	N= 268	F= 6.21	F= 1.62
	$\bar{X}$=10.41	$\bar{X}$=12.47	$\bar{X}$=14.73	$\bar{X}$=15.19	df= 3, 735	df= 2, 735
	s= 6.28	s= 7.29	s= 7.39	s= 6.67	p <.01	NS
GUTSC2E	N= 4	N= 74	N= 285	N= 376	F= 4.37	F= 1.41
	$\bar{X}$= 9.25	$\bar{X}$=11.94	$\bar{X}$=14.40	$\bar{X}$=14.94	df= 3, 735	df= 2, 735
	s= 3.40	s= 7.11	s= 7.47	s= 6.87	p <.01	NS
GUTSC3A	N= 18	N= 111	N= 322	N= 253	F= 10.87	F= .75
	$\bar{X}$=10.84	$\bar{X}$=11.72	$\bar{X}$=14.49	$\bar{X}$=15.94	df= 3, 700	df= 2, 700
	s= 7.39	s= 8.25	s= 6.67	s= 6.94	p <.01	NS
GUTSC3B	N= 32	N= 165	N= 317	N= 190	F= 14.83	F= .01
	$\bar{X}$=10.45	$\bar{X}$=12.45	$\bar{X}$=14.59	$\bar{X}$=16.74	df= 3, 700	df= 2, 700
	s= 7.69	s= 7.72	s= 6.58	s= 6.89	p <.01	NS
GUTSC3C	N= 21	N= 113	N= 343	N= 227	F= 12.44	F= .72
	$\bar{X}$=11.49	$\bar{X}$=11.69	$\bar{X}$=14.36	$\bar{X}$=16.32	df= 3, 700	df= 2, 700
	s= 7.92	s= 8.20	s= 6.45	s= 6.74	p <.01	NS
GUTSC3D	N= 36	N= 174	N= 321	N= 173	F= 16.54	F= .17
	$\bar{X}$=10.65	$\bar{X}$=12.49	$\bar{X}$=14.57	$\bar{X}$=17.11	df= 3, 700	df= 2, 700
	s= 7.99	s= 7.70	s= 6.56	s= 6.73	p <.01	NS

Table VII.6 *Sweden, Girls - Reading Comprehension Total Corrected Score*

Guttman scale	Scale types 0	1	2	3	Analysis of variance	Test of linearity
GUTSC1A	N= 30 X̄=16.03 s= 9.40	N= 202 X̄=20.44 s= 8.50	N= 301 X̄=23.76 s= 8.85	N= 179 X̄=26.60 s= 8.31	F= 23.41 df= 3, 708 p <.01	F= .36 df= 2, 708 NS
GUTSC1B	N= 37 X̄=15.89 s= 8.75	N= 231 X̄=20.35 s= 8.81	N= 304 X̄=23.93 s= 8.72	N= 140 X̄=28.27 s= 7.03	F= 35.58 df= 3, 708 p <.01	F= .19 df= 2, 708 NS
GUTSC2A	N= 6 X̄=10.67 s= 8.11	N= 70 X̄=20.66 s= 8.73	N= 319 X̄=22.72 s= 9.19	N= 344 X̄=24.34 s= 8.67	F= 8.03 df= 3, 735 p <.01	F= 2.47 df= 2, 735 NS
GUTSC2B	N= 13 X̄=13.09 s=10.06	N= 104 X̄=20.59 s= 7.93	N= 329 X̄=23.01 s=9.34	N= 293 X̄=24.74 s=8.49	F= 11.73 df= 3, 735 p <.01	F= 2.42 df= 2, 735 NS
GUTSC2C	N= 15 X̄=14.53 s=10.24	N= 134 X̄=20.99 s= 8.65	N= 322 X̄=23.19 s= 9.12	N= 268 X̄=24.75 s= 8.56	F= 10.29 df= 3, 735 p <.01	F= 1.96 df= 2, 735 NS
GUTSC2E	N= 4 X̄=12.65 s= 9.05	N= 74 X̄=19.56 s= 8.97	N= 285 X̄=22.67 s= 9.39	N= 376 X̄=24.39 s= 8.48	F= 8.59 df= 3, 735 p <.01	F= 1.09 df= 2, 735 NS
GUTSC3A	N= 18 X̄=15.68 s= 7.83	N= 111 X̄=19.20 s= 8.56	N= 322 X̄=22.57 s= 8.82	N= 253 X̄=26.70 s= 7.92	F= 28.05 df= 3, 700 p <.01	F= .19 df= 2, 700 NS
GUTSC3B	N= 32 X̄=16.14 s= 8.99	N= 165 X̄=19.20 s= 8.78	N= 317 X̄=23.48 s= 8.31	N= 190 X̄=27.93 s= 7.42	F= 41.85 df= 3, 700 p <.01	F= .31 df= 2, 700 NS
GUTSC3C	N= 21 X̄=16.38 s= 7.69	N= 113 X̄=19.27 s= 8.50	N= 343 X̄=22.69 s= 8.81	N= 227 X̄=27.01 s= 7.85	F= 28.57 df= 3, 700 p <.01	F= .45 df= 2, 700 NS
GUTSC3D	N= 36 X̄=16.53 s= 8.69	N= 174 X̄=19.27 s= 8.71	N= 321 X̄=23.77 s= 8.32	N= 173 X̄=28.08 s= 7.42	F= 41.82 df= 3, 700 p <.01	F= .49 df= 2, 700 NS

Table VII.7 *India, Boys - Science Total Corrected Score*

Guttman scale	Scale types 0	1	2	3	Analysis of variance	Test of linearity
GUTSC1A	N= 49	N= 225	N= 287	N= 145	F= 66.87	F= .78
	$\bar{X}$= 4.99	$\bar{X}$= 7.93	$\bar{X}$=11.94	$\bar{X}$=16.40	df= 3, 702	df= 2, 702
	s= 6.35	s= 6.26	s= 6.61	s= 6.50	p < .01	NS
GUTSC1B	N= 105	N= 251	N= 247	N= 103	F= 118.98	F= .42
	$\bar{X}$= 4.55	$\bar{X}$= 8.64	$\bar{X}$=13.37	$\bar{X}$=18.33	df= 3, 702	df= 2, 702
	s= 5.77	s= 5.87	s= 6.18	s= 5.85	p < .01	NS
GUTSC2A	N= 38	N= 146	N= 340	N= 191	F= 77.77	F= 2.57
	$\bar{X}$= 3.76	$\bar{X}$= 6.09	$\bar{X}$=11.62	$\bar{X}$=15.39	df= 3, 711	df= 2, 711
	s= 4.98	s= 6.05	s= 6.55	s= 6.35	p < .01	NS
GUTSC2B	N= 79	N= 164	N= 309	N= 163	F= 111.64	F= 3.53
	$\bar{X}$= 3.75	$\bar{X}$= 6.78	$\bar{X}$=12.59	$\bar{X}$=16.10	df= 3, 711	df= 2, 711
	s= 4.92	s= 6.10	s= 6.11	s= 6.19	p < .01	p < .05
GUTSC2C	N= 45	N= 223	N= 293	N= 154	F= 77.78	F= 2.09
	$\bar{X}$= 3.29	$\bar{X}$= 7.56	$\bar{X}$=12.58	$\bar{X}$=15.62	df= 3, 711	df= 2, 711
	s= 5.31	s= 7.14	s= 5.98	s= 5.96	p < .01	NS
GUTSC2E	N= 21	N= 117	N= 349	N= 228	F= 47.68	F= .58
	$\bar{X}$= 2.49	$\bar{X}$= 6.59	$\bar{X}$=10.98	$\bar{X}$=14.33	df= 3, 711	df= 2, 711
	s= 5.69	s= 6.93	s= 6.94	s= 6.10	p < .01	NS
GUTSC3A	N= 57	N= 167	N= 362	N= 105	F= 33.48	F= 3.84
	$\bar{X}$= 5.31	$\bar{X}$= 8.35	$\bar{X}$=12.55	$\bar{X}$=13.75	df= 3, 687	df= 2, 687
	s= 5.10	s= 6.32	s= 6.77	s= 8.37	p < .01	p < .05
GUTSC3B	N= 93	N= 305	N= 243	N= 50	F= 50.46	F= 4.55
	$\bar{X}$= 4.67	$\bar{X}$=10.34	$\bar{X}$=13.62	$\bar{X}$=15.68	df= 3, 687	df= 2, 687
	s= 5.21	s= 6.05	s= 7.32	s= 8.31	p < .01	p < .05
GUTSC3C	N= 64	N= 180	N= 369	N= 78	F= 43.74	F= .82
	$\bar{X}$= 5.44	$\bar{X}$= 8.25	$\bar{X}$=12.55	$\bar{X}$=15.60	df= 3, 687	df= 2, 687
	s= 5.22	s= 6.26	s= 6.89	s= 7.67	p < .01	NS
GUTSC3D	N= 104	N= 327	N= 220	N= 40	F= 66.87	F= 2.89
	$\bar{X}$= 4.78	$\bar{X}$=10.16	$\bar{X}$=14.51	$\bar{X}$=16.73	df= 3, 687	df= 2, 687
	s= 5.27	s= 6.01	s= 7.32	s= 7.08	p < .01	NS

Table VII.8 *India, Boys - Word Knowledge Total Corrected Score*

Guttman scale	Scale types 0	1	2	3	Analysis of variance	Test of linearity
GUTSC1A	N= 49	N= 225	N= 287	N= 145	F= 26.10	F= .31
	$\bar{X}$= 9.15	$\bar{X}$=13.19	$\bar{X}$=16.55	$\bar{X}$=21.16	df= 3, 702	df= 2, 702
	s= 7.66	s=10.78	s=10.32	s= 9.34	p <.01	NS
GUTSC1B	N= 105	N= 251	N= 247	N= 103	F= 35.14	F= 1.00
	$\bar{X}$= 9.20	$\bar{X}$=14.45	$\bar{X}$=17.49	$\bar{X}$=22.55	df= 3, 702	df= 2, 702
	s= 7.18	s=10.91	s=10.19	s= 9.27	p <.01	NS
GUTSC2A	N= 38	N= 146	N= 340	N= 191	F= 40.96	F= 2.54
	$\bar{X}$= 7.75	$\bar{X}$=10.12	$\bar{X}$=16.89	$\bar{X}$=20.54	df= 3, 711	df= 2, 711
	s= 6.87	s= 8.00	s=10.64	s=10.02	p <.01	NS
GUTSC2B	N= 79	N= 164	N= 309	N= 163	F= 52.64	F= 5.19
	$\bar{X}$= 8.54	$\bar{X}$=10.64	$\bar{X}$=18.09	$\bar{X}$=21.03	df= 3, 711	df= 2, 711
	s= 6.68	s= 8.79	s=10.42	s=10.00	p <.01	p <.01
GUTSC2C	N= 45	N= 223	N= 293	N= 154	F= 32.20	F= 1.69
	$\bar{X}$= 7.68	$\bar{X}$=12.46	$\bar{X}$=17.71	$\bar{X}$=20.29	df= 3, 711	df= 2, 711
	s= 6.77	s= 9.66	s=10.61	s= 9.93	p <.01	NS
GUTSC2E	N= 21	N= 117	N= 349	N= 228	F= 19.14	F= 4.95
	$\bar{X}$= 8.68	$\bar{X}$=10.50	$\bar{X}$=16.85	$\bar{X}$=18.18	df= 3, 711	df= 2, 711
	s= 7.75	s= 8.37	s=10.82	s=10.33	p <.01	p <.01
GUTSC3A	N= 57	N= 167	N= 362	N= 105	F= 24.38	F= 4.54
	$\bar{X}$= 8.71	$\bar{X}$=12.16	$\bar{X}$=17.92	$\bar{X}$=18.74	df= 3, 687	df= 2, 687
	s= 8.46	s= 9.18	s=10.52	s=11.34	p <.01	p <.05
GUTSC3B	N= 93	N= 305	N= 243	N= 50	F= 17.37	F= 9.18
	$\bar{X}$= 8.86	$\bar{X}$=16.51	$\bar{X}$=17.20	$\bar{X}$=18.85	df= 3, 687	df= 2, 687
	s= 8.52	s=10.26	s=10.85	s=11.24	p <.01	p <.01
GUTSC3C	N= 64	N= 180	N= 369	N= 78	F= 25.77	F= 2.83
	$\bar{X}$= 9.01	$\bar{X}$=12.37	$\bar{X}$=18.03	$\bar{X}$=19.55	df= 3, 687	df= 2, 687
	s= 8.29	s= 9.38	s=10.37	s=12.12	p <.01	NS
GUTSC3D	N= 104	N= 327	N= 220	N= 40	F= 18.19	F= 8.01
	$\bar{X}$= 9.20	$\bar{X}$=16.47	$\bar{X}$=17.64	$\bar{X}$=18.96	df= 3, 687	df= 2, 687
	s= 8.47	s=10.17	s=11.10	s=11.39	p <.01	p <.01

Table VII.9 *India, Boys - Reading Comprehension Total Corrected Score*

Guttman scale	Scale types				Analysis of variance	Test of linearity
	0	1	2	3		
GUTSC1A	N= 49	N= 225	N= 287	N= 145	F= 9.16	F= .76
	$\bar{X}$= 9.18	$\bar{X}$=11.83	$\bar{X}$=14.01	$\bar{X}$=14.99	df= 3, 702	df= 2, 702
	s= 5.97	s= 8.01	s= 8.93	s= 7.89	$p < .01$	NS
GUTSC1B	N= 105	N= 251	N= 247	N= 103	F= 21.89	F= 2.10
	$\bar{X}$= 9.23	$\bar{X}$=11.58	$\bar{X}$=15.27	$\bar{X}$=16.12	df= 3, 702	df= 2, 702
	s= 5.91	s= 8.02	s= 8.81	s= 8.08	$p < .01$	NS
GUTSC2A	N= 38	N= 146	N= 340	N= 191	F= 21.10	F= 2.45
	$\bar{X}$= 8.99	$\bar{X}$= 9.54	$\bar{X}$=13.85	$\bar{X}$=15.81	df= 3, 711	df= 2, 711
	s= 6.15	s= 6.34	s= 8.72	s= 8.20	$p < .01$	NS
GUTSC2B	N= 79	N= 164	N= 309	N= 163	F= 31.38	F= 3.86
	$\bar{X}$= 8.84	$\bar{X}$= 9.67	$\bar{X}$=14.55	$\bar{X}$=16.46	df= 3, 711	df= 2, 711
	s= 6.04	s= 6.37	s= 8.89	s= 7.94	$p < .01$	$p < .05$
GUTSC2C	N= 45	N= 223	N= 293	N= 154	F= 22.23	F= 1.46
	$\bar{X}$= 9.02	$\bar{X}$=10.50	$\bar{X}$=14.35	$\bar{X}$=16.30	df= 3, 711	df= 2, 711
	s= 6.44	s= 6.89	s= 8.83	s= 8.28	$p < .01$	NS
GUTSC2E	N= 21	N= 117	N= 349	N= 228	F= 8.18	F= .56
	$\bar{X}$= 7.81	$\bar{X}$=11.10	$\bar{X}$=13.30	$\bar{X}$=14.73	df= 3, 711	df= 2, 711
	s= 6.08	s= 6.49	s= 8.79	s= 8.30	$p < .01$	NS
GUTSC3A	N= 57	N= 167	N= 362	N= 105	F= 17.23	F= 1.37
	$\bar{X}$= 9.00	$\bar{X}$=10.71	$\bar{X}$=14.41	$\bar{X}$=15.99	df= 3, 687	df= 2, 687
	s= 5.15	s= 6.20	s= 8.91	s= 8.97	$p < .01$	NS
GUTSC3B	N= 93	N= 305	N= 243	N= 50	F= 9.38	F= 4.60
	$\bar{X}$= 9.77	$\bar{X}$=13.60	$\bar{X}$=13.52	$\bar{X}$=17.05	df= 3, 687	df= 2, 687
	s= 5.74	s= 8.99	s= 8.18	s= 7.32	$p < .01$	$p < .05$
GUTSC3C	N= 64	N= 180	N= 369	N= 78	F= 19.57	F= .52
	$\bar{X}$= 8.95	$\bar{X}$=10.91	$\bar{X}$=14.45	$\bar{X}$=17.01	df= 3, 687	df= 2, 687
	s= 5.34	s= 6.19	s= 8.90	s= 9.32	$p < .01$	NS
GUTSC3D	N= 104	N= 327	N= 220	N= 40	F= 9.92	F= 3.06
	$\bar{X}$= 9.73	$\bar{X}$=13.51	$\bar{X}$=14.03	$\bar{X}$=16.99	df= 3, 687	df= 2, 687
	s= 5.94	s= 8.81	s= 8.26	s= 7.85	$p < .01$	$p < .05$

Appendix VII

Figures – Relative Frequencies and Trends of Ten Guttman Scales

Dependent Variables: Science Total Corrected Score (SCAB), Word Knowledge Total Corrected Score (WKC), Reading Comprehension Total Corrected Score (RCC)
(Samples and Scale Names are given in Table Headings)

Figure VII.1 *Sweden Total and India Boys - GUTSC1A, GUTSC1B*

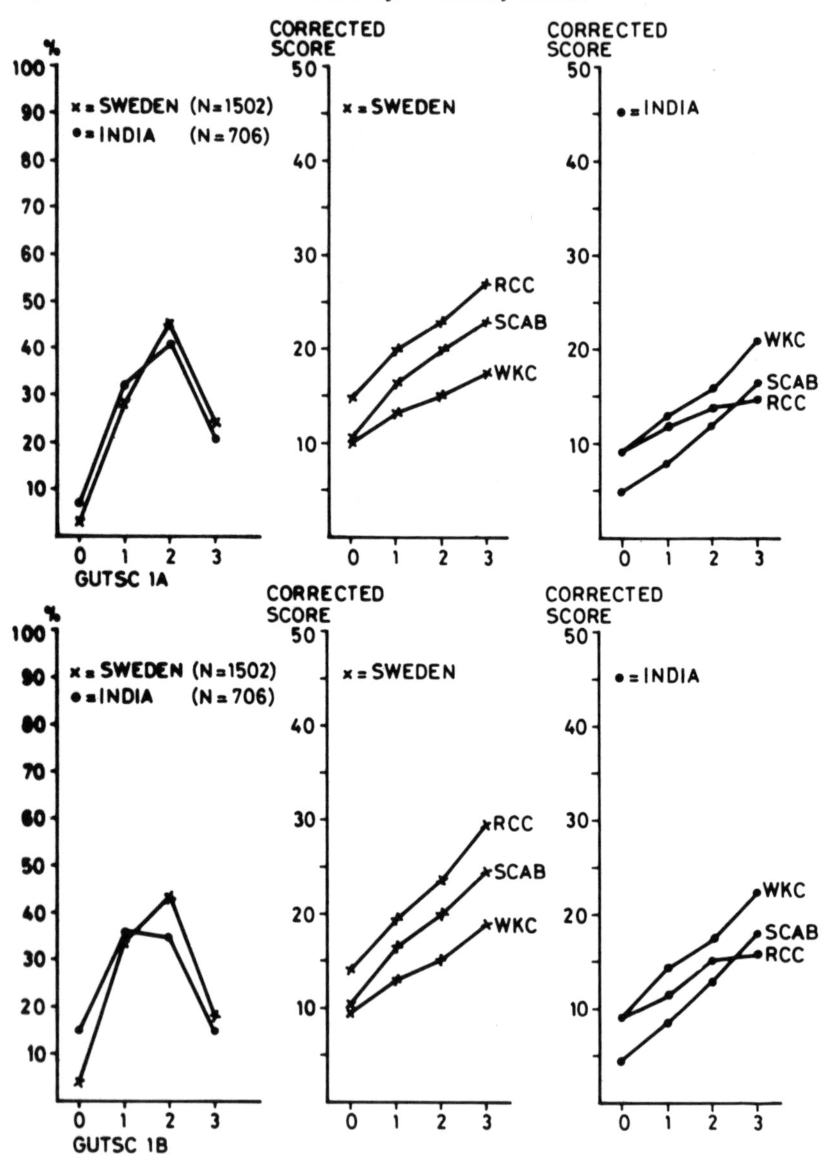

Figure VII.2 *Sweden Total and India Boys - GUTSC2A, GUTSC2B*

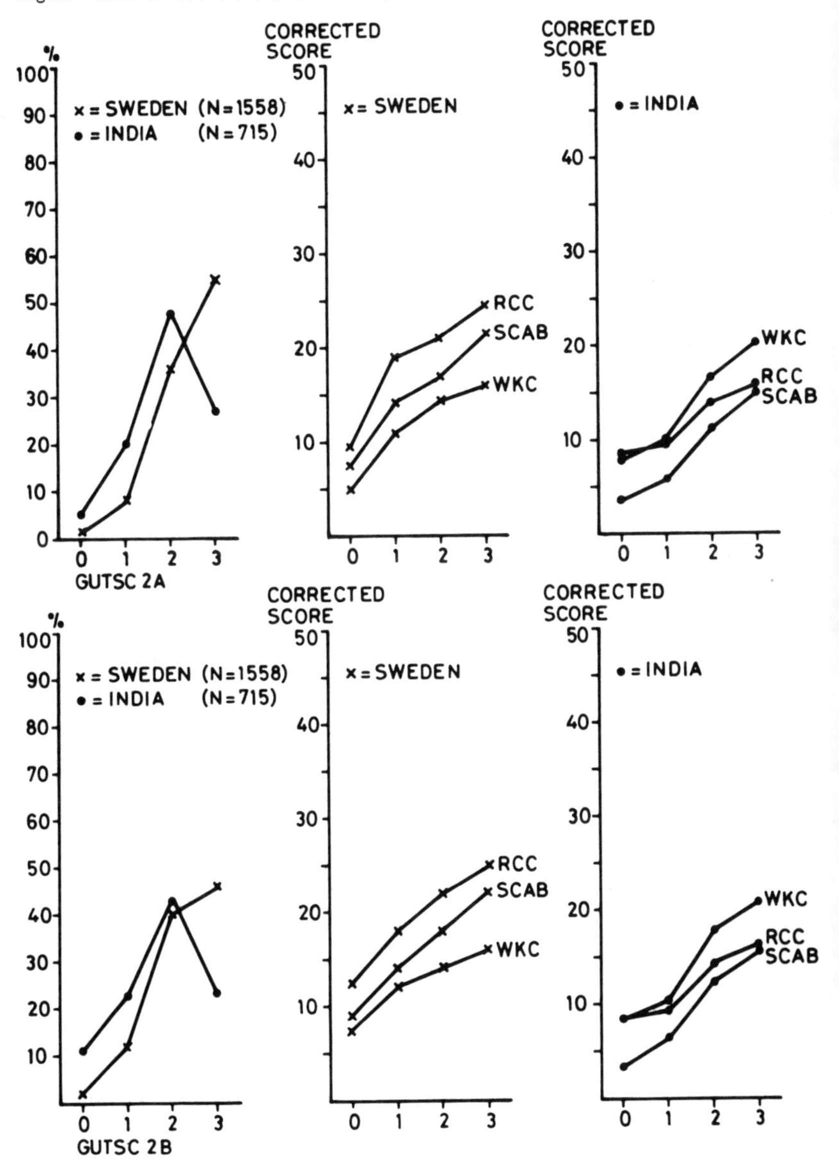

Figure VII.3 *Sweden Total and India Boys - GUTSC2C, GUTSC2E*

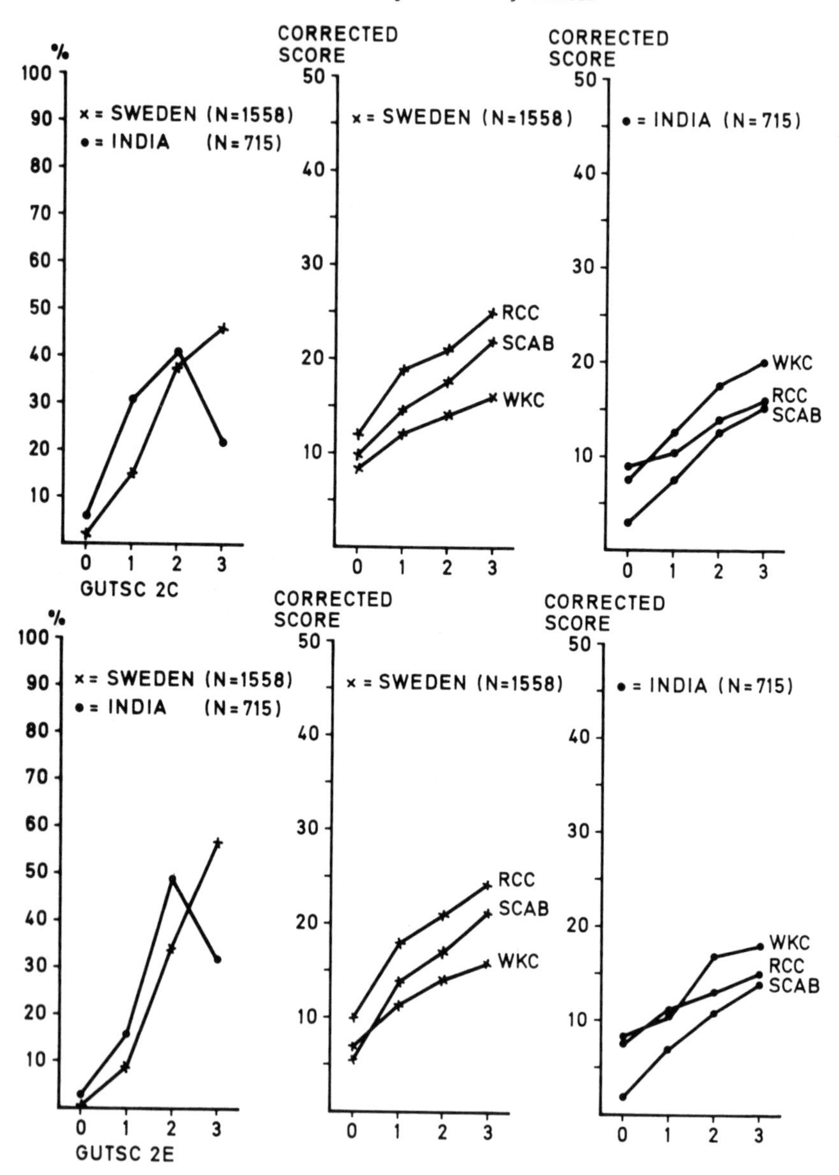

Figure VII.4 *Sweden Total and India Boys - GUTSC3A, GUTSC3B*

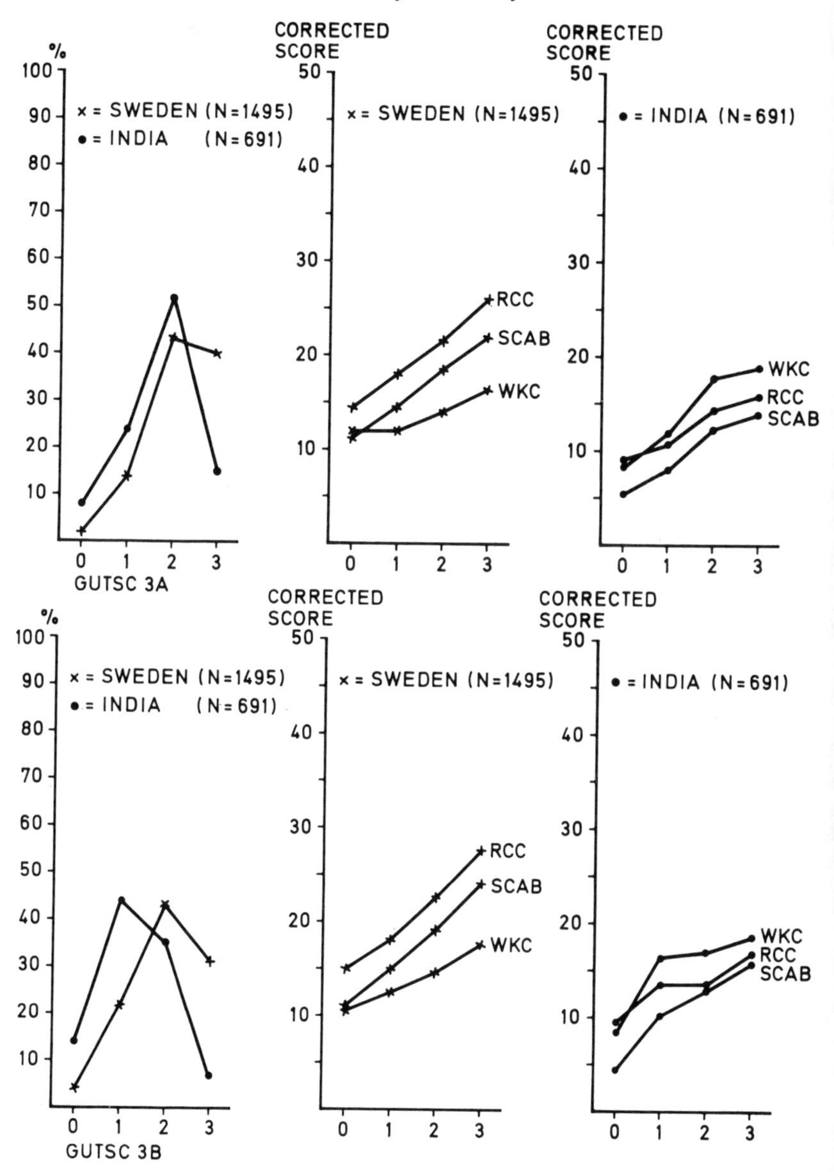

Figure VII.5 *Sweden Total and India Boys - GUTSC3C, GUTSC3D*

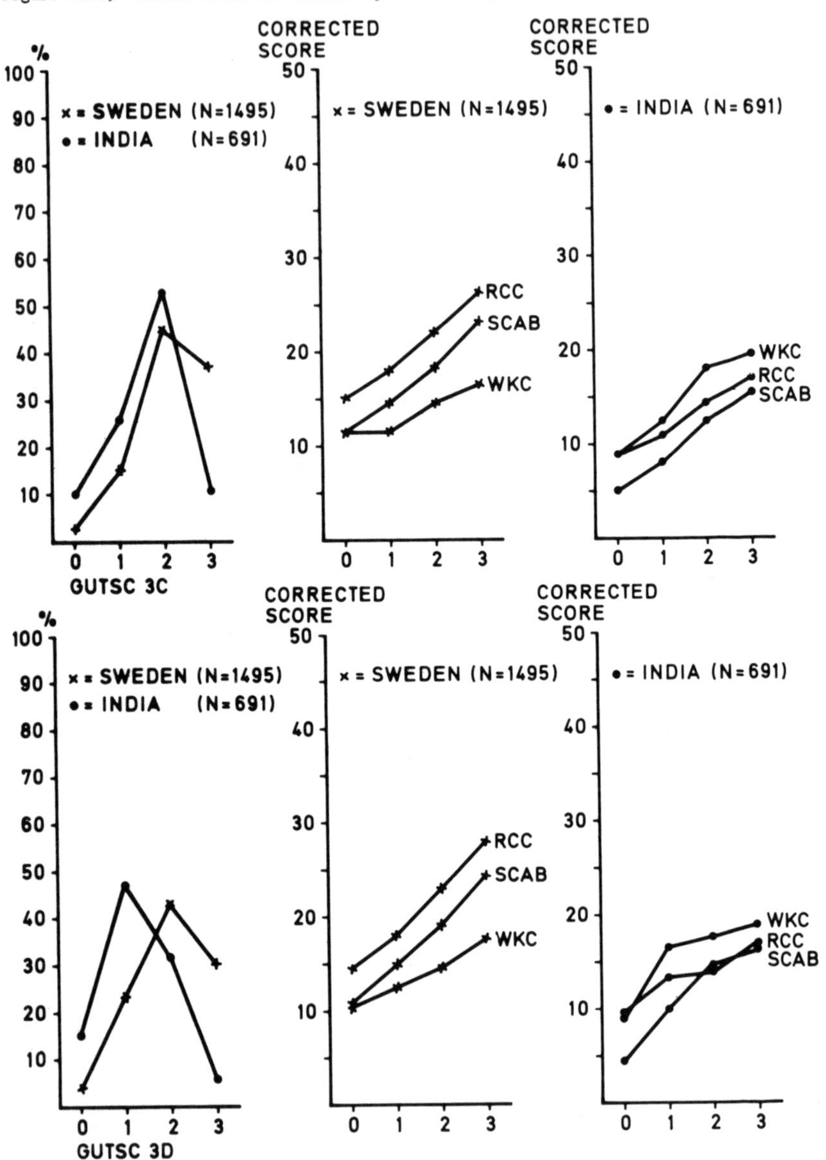

Figure VII.6 *Sweden Boys and Sweden Girls - GUTSC1A, GUTSC1B*

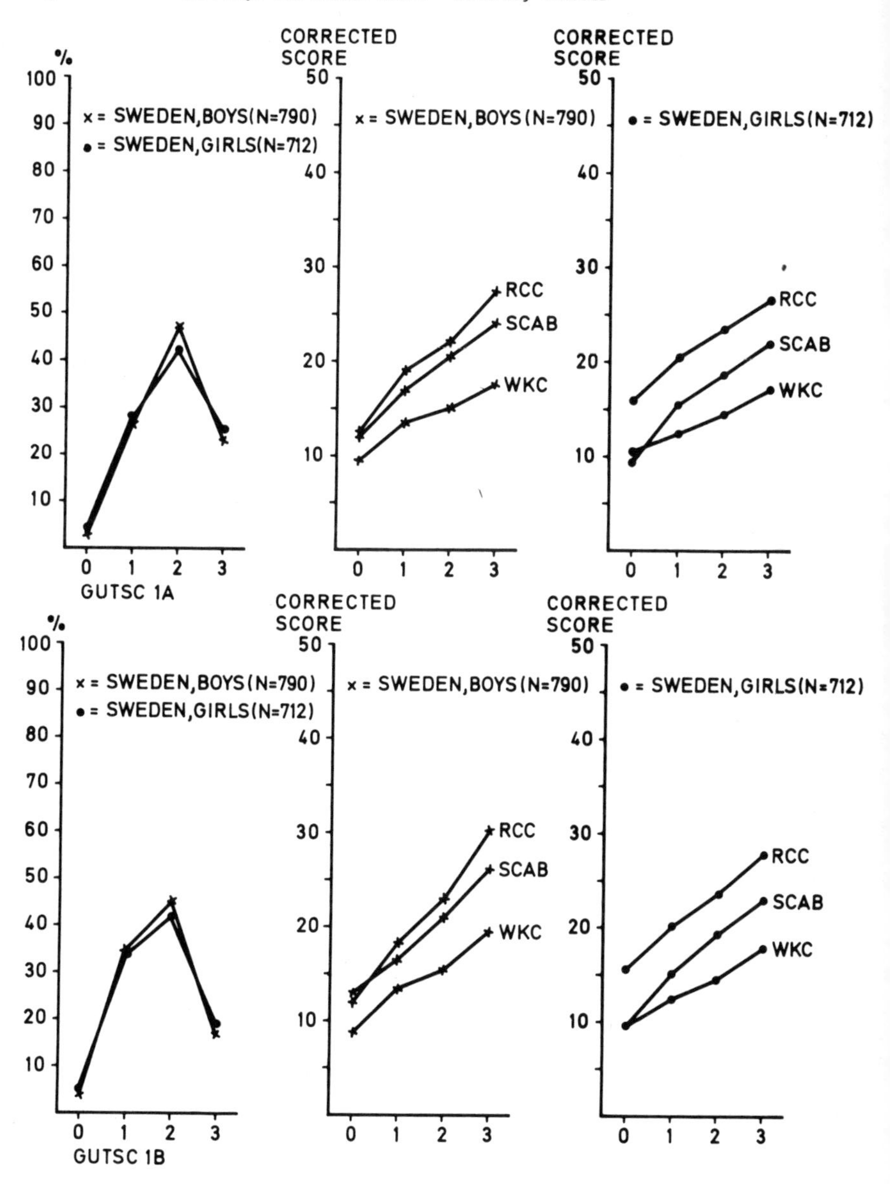

Figure VII.7 *Sweden Boys and Sweden Girls - GUTSC2A, GUTSC2B*

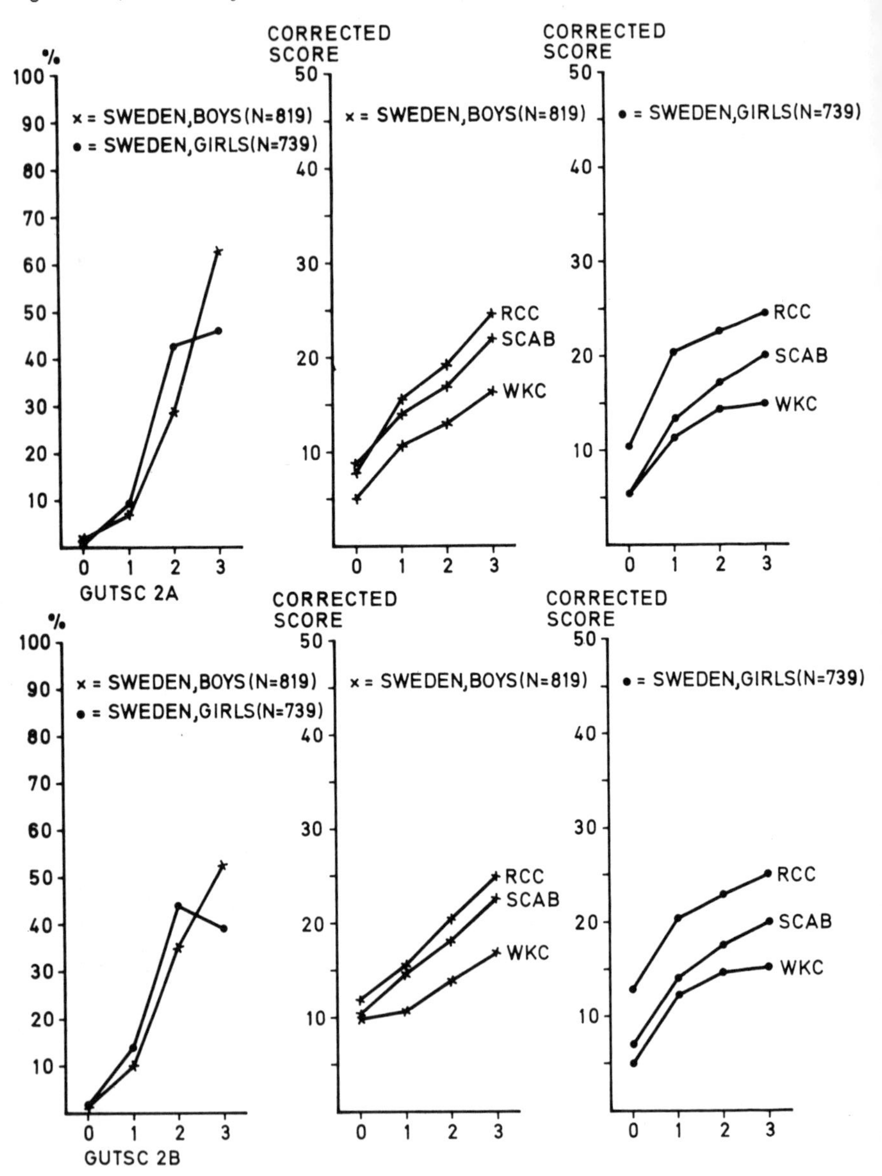

Figure VII.8 *Sweden Boys and Sweden Girls - GUTSC2C, GUTSC2E*

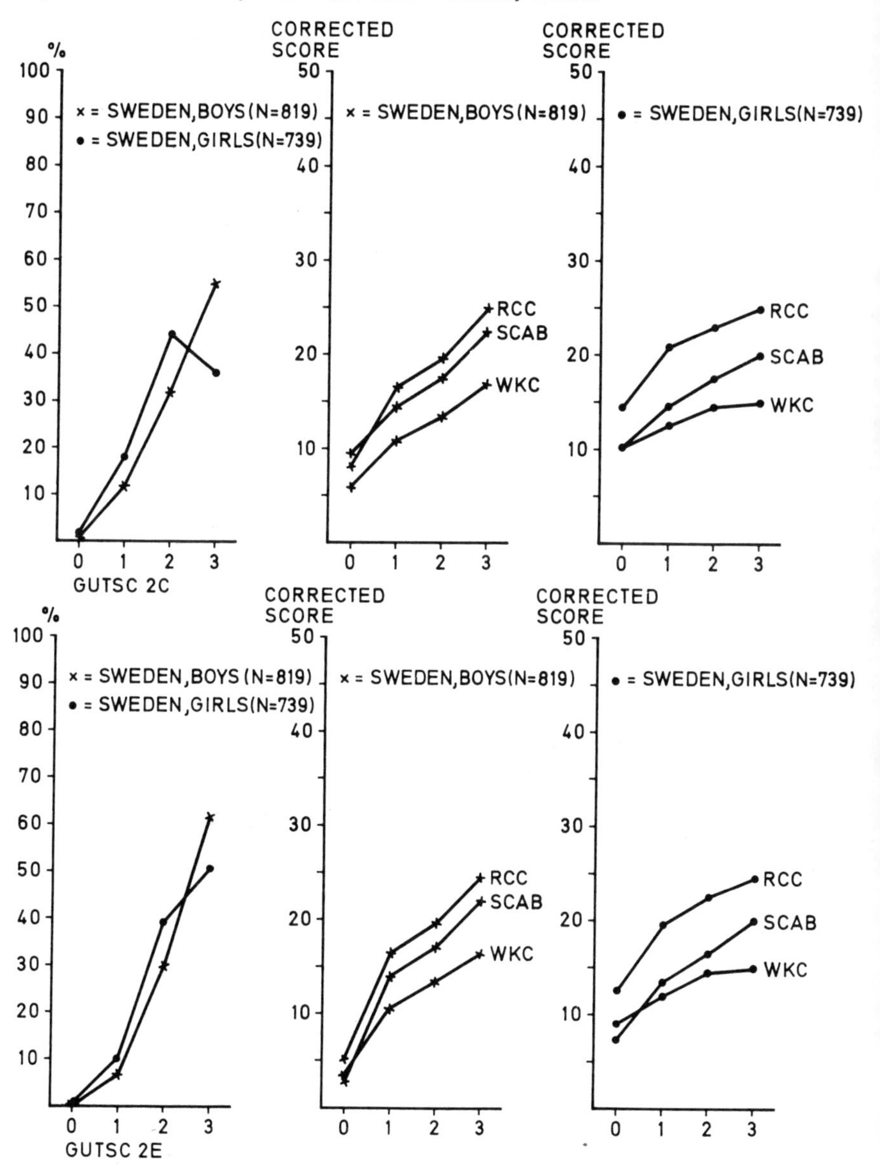

Figure VII.9 *Sweden Boys and Sweden Girls - GUTSC3A, GUTSC3B*

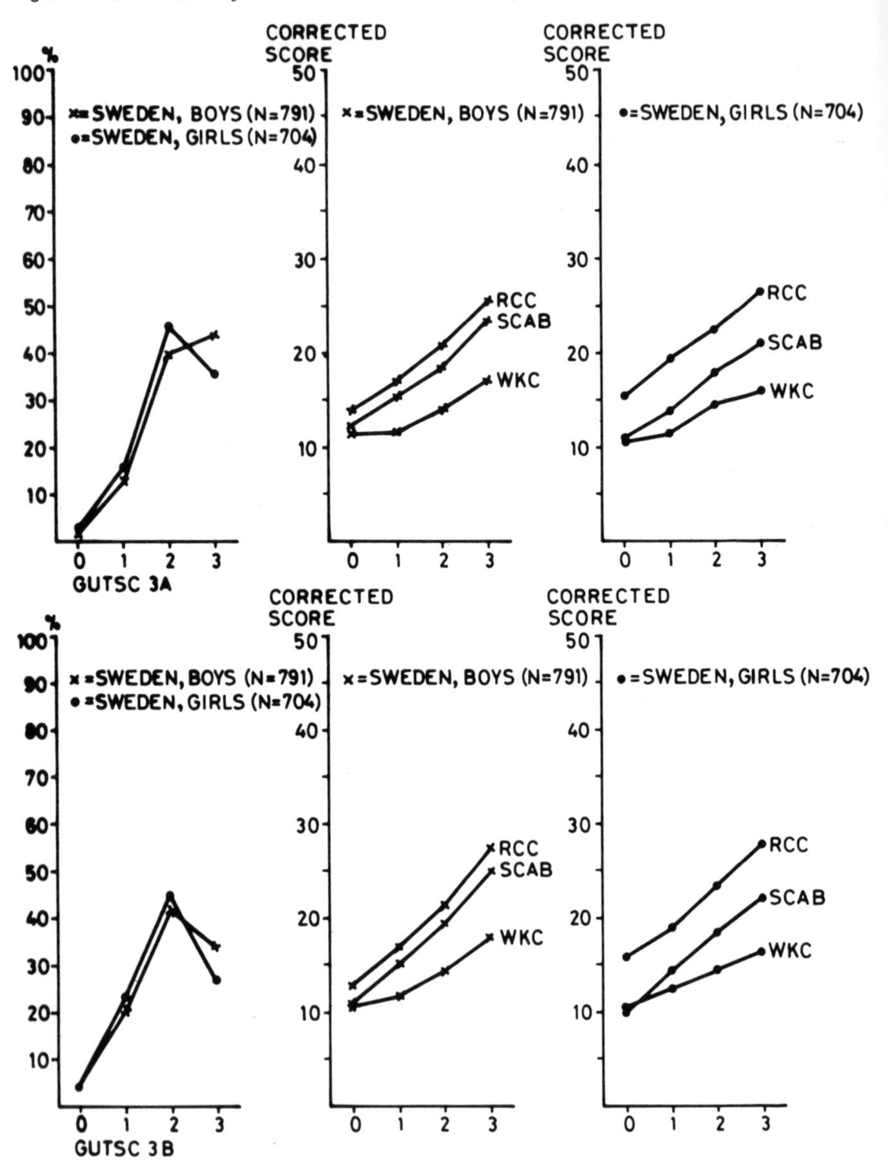

Figure VII.10 *Sweden Boys and Sweden Girls - GUTSC3C, GUTSC3D*

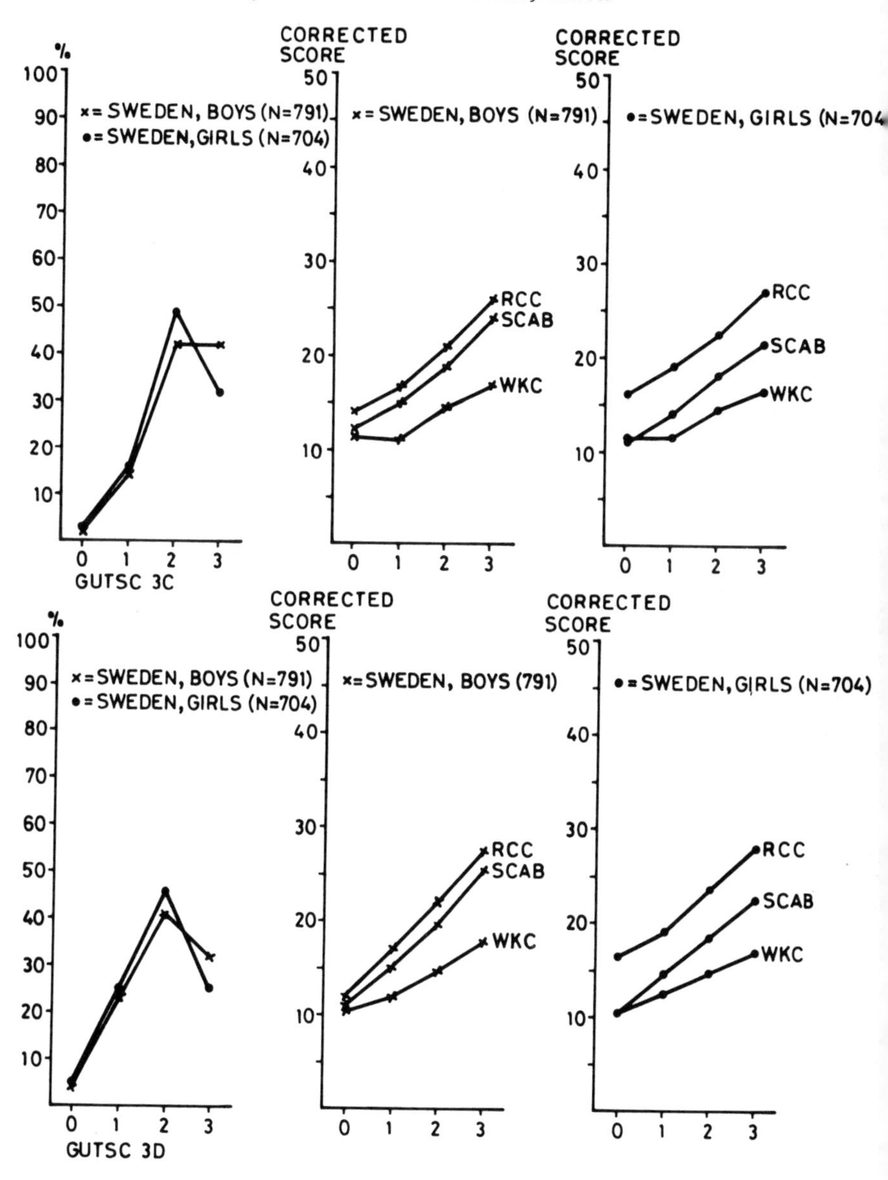

REFERENCES

Anderson, R.E. "A Computer Program for Guttman Scaling with the Goudenough Technique." *Behavioral Science,* 11(3): 235, 1966.

Bergling, K. *Begreppsbildning.* (Concept formation.) Stockholm School of Education, 1971.

Bloom, B.S. *Cross-National Study of Educational Attainment: Stage I of the IEA Investigation in Six Subject Areas.* Washington D.C.: US Department of Health, Education and Welfare, Office of Education. Final Report Project No. 6–2527, 1969.

Comber, L.C. and Keeves, J.P. *Science Education in Nineteen Countries.* International Studies in Evaluation I. New York: John Wiley; Stockholm: Almqvist & Wiksell, 1973.

Cronbach, L.J. *Essentials of Psychological Testing.* (3rd edition.) New York: Harper & Row, 1970.

Cronbach, L.J. "Test Validation." In R.L. Thorndike (Ed.), *Educational Measurement, Second Edition.* Washington: American Council on Education, 1971. pp. 443–507.

Cronbach, L.J. and Drenth, P.J.D. (Eds.) *Mental Tests and Cultural Adaptation.* Psychological Studies 7. Paris: Mouton, 1972.

Cronbach, L.J. and Meehl, P.E. "Construct Validity in Psychological Tests." *Psychological Bulletin,* 52: 281–302, 1955.

Cureton, E.E. "Validity." In E.F. Lindquist (Ed.), *Educational Measurement.* Washington: American Council of Education 1951. pp. 621–694.

Dodwell, P.C. "Children's Understanding of Number and Related Concepts." *Canadian Journal of Psychology,* 14: 191–205, 1960.

Dodwell, P.C. "Children's Understanding of Number Concepts: Characteristics of an Individual and of a Group Test." *Canadian Journal of Psychology,* 15: 29–36, 1961.

Dodwell, P.C. "Relations between the Understanding of the Logic of Classes and of Cardinal Number in Children." *Canadian Journal of Psychology,* 16(2): 152–160, 1962.

Dodwell, P.C. "Children's Understanding of Spatial Concepts." *Canadian Journal of Psychology,* 17(1): 141–161, 1963.

Ebel, R.L. "Writing the Test Item." In E.F. Lindquist (Ed.), *Educational Measurement.* Washington, D.C.: American Council of Education, 1951. pp. 185–249.

Eckensberger, L.H. "The Necessity of a Theory for Applied Crosscultural Research." In L.J. Cronbach and P.J.D. Drenth (Eds.) *Mental Tests and Cultural Adaptation.* Paris: Mouton, 1972. pp. 99–107.

Ekman, G. *Reliabilitet och konstans. Ett bidrag till testpsykologiens metodologi.* Uppsala: Gebers, 1947.

Ferguson, G.A. *Statistical Analysis in Psychology and Education.* New York: McGraw-Hill, 1966.

Flavell, J.H. *The Developmental Psychology of Jean Piaget.* With a Foreword by Jean Piaget. New York: Van Nostrand Reinhold, 1963.

Fogelman, K.R. "Difficulties of Using Piagetian Tests in the Classroom—I." *Educational Research*, 12(1): 36–40, 1969.

Foshay, A.W. *Educational Achievement of Thirteen-Year-Olds in Twelve Countries.* Hamburg: Unesco Institute for Education, 1962.

Goldman, R. *Religious Thinking from Childhood to Adolescence.* London: Routledge & Kegan Paul, 1964.

Goldschmid, M.L. and Bentler, P.M. "The Dimensions and Measurement of Conservation." *Child Development,* 39(3), 787–802, 1968.

Guttman, L. "A Basis for Scaling Qualitative Data." *American Sociological Review,* 9: 139–150, 1944.

Guttman, L. Chapters 2, 3, 6, 8. In: S.A. Stouffer, *et al.* (Eds.) *Measurement and Prediction.* Princeton: Princeton University Press, 1950.

Hunt, J.McV. *Intelligence and Experience.* New York: Ronald Press, 1961.

Husén, T. (Ed.) *International Study of Achievement in Mathematics.* Stockholm: Almqvist & Wiksell; New York: John Wiley & Sons, 1967.

Husén, T. *et al. Svensk skola i internationell belysning I, Naturorienterande ämnen.* Stockholm: Almqvist & Wiksell, 1973.

Husén, T. Multi-National Evaluation of School Systems: Purposes, Methodology, and Some Preliminary Findings. *Scandinavian Journal of Educational Research,* 18: 13–39, 1974.

Inhelder, B. and Piaget, J. *The Early Growth of Logic in the Child. Classification and seriation.* London: Routledge and Kegan Paul, 1964.

Inhelder, B. and Piaget, J. *The Growth of Logical Thinking from Childhood to Adolescence.* London: Routledge & Kegan Paul, 1958.

Lieberman, M. "Estimation of a Moral Judgment Level using Items whose Alternatives form a Graded Scale." *ED 048 341,* 1971.

Manual for Test Administrators. (IEA/M3).

Mannix, J.B. "The Number Concept of a Group of E.S.N. Children." *British Journal of Educational Psychology, 30:180–181, 1960.*

Martinsson, S. *Religionsundervisning och mognad.* (Religious Education and Readiness. A study of the ability of abstract thinking and understanding of parables and religious symbols.) Stockholm School of Education, 1968.

Mays, W. "An Elementary Introduction to Piaget's Logic." In J. Piaget, *Logic and Psychology,* Manchester: Manchester University Press, 1956. pp. ix–xvi.

Nie, N.H., Bent, D.H. and Hull, C.H. *Statistical Package for the Social Sciences.* New York: McGraw-Hill, 1970.

Peaker, G.F. (Forthcoming) *An Empirical Study of Education in Twenty-one Countries: A Technical Report.* Stockholm: Almqvist & Wiksell.

Pettersson, S. *Mognad och abstrakt stoff.* (Readiness and Abstract Learning). Stockholm School of Education, 1970.

Piaget, J. *Traité de logique.* Paris: Colin, 1949.

Piaget, J. *The psychology of Intelligence.* New York: Harcourt, Brace, 1950.

Piaget, J. *The Child's Conception of Number.* New York: Humanities, 1952.

Piaget, J. *Logic and Psychology.* Manchester: Manchester University Press, 1956.

Piaget, J. "Nécessité et signification des rechereches comparatives en psychologie

génétique." *International Journal of Psychology*, 1(1): 3–13, 1966.
Raven, R.J. "The Development of a Test of Piaget's Logical Operations." *Science Education*, 57(3): 377–385, 1973.
Schuessler, K. and Strauss, A. "A Study of Concept Learning by Scale Analysis." *American Sociological Review*, 15:752–762, 1950.
Schwartz, M.M. and Scholnick, E.K. "Scalogram Analysis of Logical and Perceptual Components of Conservation of Discontinuous Quantity." *Child Development*, 41: 695–705, 1970.
Stephens, B., Manhanley, E.J. and McLaughlin, J.A. "Mental Ages for Achievement of Piagetian Reasoning Assessments." *Education and Training of the Mentally Retarded*, 7: 124–128, 1972.
Strauss, A. and Schuessler, K. "Socialization, Logical Reasoning, and Concept Development in the Child." *American Sociological Review*, 16: 514–523, 1951.
Thorndike, R.L. *Reading Comprehension Education in Fifteen Countries*. International Studies in Evaluation III. New York: John Wiley; Stockholm: Almqvist & Wiksell, 1973.
Tisher, R.P. "A Piagetian Questionnaire Applied to Pupils in a Secondary School." *Child Development*, 42: 1633–1636, 1971.
Weinstein, E.A. "Development of the Concept of Flag and the Sense of National Identity. *Child Development*, 28: 167–174, 1957.
Weisman, L.I. and Safford, P.L. "Piagetian Tasks as Classroom Evaluative Tools." *Elementary School Journal*, 71(6):329–338, 1971.
Wesman, A.G., and Bennett, G.K. "The Use of 'None of These' as an Option in Test Construction." *Journal of Educational Psychology*, 37: 541–554, 1946.
Wesman, A.G. "Writing the Test Item." In R.L. Thorndike (Ed.), *Educational Measurement*, (2nd ed.) Washington, D.C.: American Council on Education, 1971. pp. 81–129.
Winer, B.J. *Statistical Principles in Experimental Design*. New York: McGraw-Hill, 1970.
Wohlwill, J.F. A Study of the Development of the Number Concept by Scalogram Analysis. *Journal of Genetic Psychology*, 97: 345:377, 1960.
Zern, D. "Some Trends in the Development of Concrete Reasoning in Children": a note to Jan Smedslund's "Concrete Reasoning: A Study of Intellectual Development." *Journal of Genetic Psychology*, 115: 3–5, 1969.

I E A International Studies in Evaluation

I. Comber, L.C. and Keeves, J.P., *Science Education in Nineteen Countries: An Empirical Study*. Stockholm: Almqvist & Wiksell, 1973.

II. Purves, A.C., *Literature Education in Ten Countries: An Empirical Study*. Stockholm: Almqvist & Wiksell, 1973.

III. Thorndike, R.L., *Reading Comprehension Education in Fifteen Countries: An Empirical Study*. Stockholm: Almqvist & Wiksell, 1973.

IV. Lewis, E.G. and Massad, C.E., *English as a Foreign Language in Ten Countries: An Empirical Study*. Stockholm: Almqvist & Wiksell (In press).

V. Carrol, J.B., *French as a Foreign Language in Eight Countries: An Empirical Study*. Stockholm: Almqvist & Wiksell (In press).

Forthcoming Reports:

Civic Education in Ten Countries: An Empirical Study.

The National Case Study: An Empirical Comparative Study of Twentyone Educational Systems

An Empirical Study of Education in Twenty-one Countries: A Technical Report

The I E A Six Subject Survey: An Empirical Study of Education in Twenty-one Countries

I E A Monograph Studies

1. Rosenshine, B., *Teaching Behaviours and Student Achievement*. London: National Foundation for Educational Research in England and Wales, 1971.
2. Oppenheim, A.N. and Torney, J.V., *The Measurement of Children's Civic Attitudes in Different Nations*. Stockholm: Almqvist & Wiksell, 1974.
3. Bergling, K., *The Development of Hypothetico-deductive Thinking in Children: A Cross-cultural Study of the Validity of Piaget's Model of the Development of Logical Thinking*. Stockholm: Almqvist & Wiksell, 1974.